Word Games

6–8

Written by
Linda Schwartz

Editors: Carla Hamaguchi and Collene Dobelmann
Illustrator: Dimension
Designer/Production: Moonhee Pak/Rosa Gandara
Cover Designer: Barbara Peterson
Art Director: Tom Cochrane
Project Director: Carolea Williams

Table of Contents

Introduction

Each book in the *Power Practice*™ series contains dozens of ready-to-use activity pages to provide students with skill practice. Use the fun activities to supplement and enhance what you are already teaching in your classroom. Give an activity page to students as independent class work, or send the pages home as homework to reinforce skills taught in class. An answer key is provided for quick reference.

Word Games 6–8 is filled with challenging puzzles and word games to help students improve their vocabulary and spelling, as well as sharpen their creative thinking skills. On many of the pages, a Just for Fun activity is provided for extended learning. The book is divided into nine main sections:

- **Make-a-Word Puzzles**
  Students go from letter to letter in adjacent circles or squares to see how many words they can make.

- **Hidden Word Puzzles**
  Students are given a three-letter word such as *ant*, *pen*, or *rat*. They write longer words that have the letter combination at the beginning, middle, or end of the word.

- **Word Search Puzzles**
  The word search puzzles are correlated to science and social studies topics. Students find and circle hidden words going forward, backward, up, down, and diagonally. Each puzzle also features an extended learning activity.

- **Category Games**
  Students list words beginning with specific letters of the alphabet for five categories. They are encouraged to use reference materials to find names of unusual mountains, rivers, authors, etc. Students can exchange game sheets and easily check answers.

- **Crossword Puzzles**
  The crossword puzzles are correlated to parts of speech, synonyms, antonyms, homophones, plurals, abbreviations, and holidays.

- **What Would You Do?**
  These humorous puzzle sheets get students into the dictionary to look up unusual words.

- **Ladder Links**
  Students change one word at the top of the ladder into another word at the bottom of the ladder by changing only one letter at a time. Definition clues help them solve the puzzles.

- **Analogies**
  Students solve analogies to better understand the relationship between pairs of words, and, at the same time, strengthen their vocabulary.

- **Fun With Words**
  This is a collection of puzzles, including anagrams, classifying games, word scrambles, and more!

Use these ready-to-go activities to "recharge" skill review and give students the power to succeed!

Word Square #1

Vocabulary and Spelling

How many words can you find in the square? Write the words you find on a separate sheet of paper. *Hint: There are more than 70 words.*

Rules

- The words you find must have four or more letters.
- Start on any square and move one square in any direction to spell a word. You may not skip a square.

  Examples: *Fist* is allowed because each square is touching another square.
  Note is not allowed because the squares with the letters *t* and *e* are not touching each other.

- You may not use the same letter twice in a row (e.g., *noon*), but you can go back and use a letter again in the same word (e.g., *none*).
- Plurals are allowed.

F	M	B	L
I	S	O	N
C	T	R	E
U	Y	A	G

Name _____ Date _____

Word Square #2

Vocabulary and Spelling

How many words can you find in the square? Write the words you find on a separate sheet of paper. *Hint: There are more than 75 words.*

Rules

- The words you find must have four or more letters.
- Start on any square and move one square in any direction to spell a word. You may not skip a square.

  Examples: *Wane* is allowed because each square is touching another square.
  Quit is not allowed because the squares with the letters *i* and *t* are not touching each other.

- You may not use the same letter twice in a row *(e.g., will)*, but you can go back and use a letter again in the same word *(e.g., nine)*.
- Plurals are allowed.

Q	Z	L	O
U	I	G	E
W	A	N	S
T	R	C	K

Word Games • 6–8 © 2005 Creative Teaching Press

Name _____ Date _____

Word Square #3

Vocabulary and Spelling

How many words can you find in the square? Write the words you find on a separate sheet of paper.
*Hint: There are more than **75** words.*

Rules

- The words you find must have four or more letters.
- Start on any square and move one square in any direction to spell a word. You may not skip a square.

    Examples: *Ants* is allowed because each square is touching another square.
    Wink is not allowed because the squares with the letters *n* and k are not touching each other.

- You may not use the same letter twice in a row *(e.g., soot)*, but you can go back and use a letter again in the same word *(e.g., tent)*.
- Plurals are allowed.

C	N	A	O
H	E	T	S
B	U	R	Y
L	K	I	W

Word Square #4

Vocabulary and Spelling

How many words can you find in the square? Write the words you find on a separate sheet of paper. *Hint: There are more than 85 words.*

Rules
- The words you find must have four or more letters.
- Start on any square and move one square in any direction to spell a word. You may not skip a square.

  Examples: *Sink* is allowed because each square is touching another square.

  Sister is not allowed because the squares with the letters *t* and *e* are not touching each other.
- You may not use the same letter twice in a row *(e.g., need)*, but you can go back and use a letter again in the same word *(e.g., gene)*.
- Plurals are allowed.

P	T	R	W
A	I	S	K
X	G	N	U
L	E	D	J

Word Games • 6–8 © 2005 Creative Teaching Press

Round and Round

Vocabulary and Spelling

How many words can you find in the circles? Write the words you find on a separate sheet of paper.
*Hint: There are more than **50** words.*

Rules

- The words you find must have three or more letters.
- Start on any circle and move to an adjacent circle connected by a line to spell a word.
  You may not skip a circle.

          Examples: *Man* is allowed because each circle is connected by a line.

                 Men is not allowed because the letter *m* is not connected to the letter *e*.

- You may not use the same letter twice in a row *(e.g., pall)*, but you can go back and use a letter again in the same word *(e.g., canal)*.

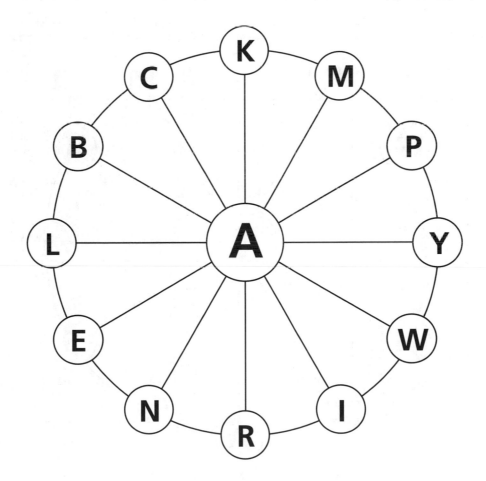

Round and Round Again

Vocabulary and Spelling

How many words can you find in the circles? Write the words you find on a separate sheet of paper. *Hint: There are more than 75 words.*

Rules
- The words you find must have three or more letters.
- Start on any circle and move to an adjacent circle connected by a line to spell a word. You may not skip a circle.
  Examples: *Hem* is allowed because each circle is connected by a line.
  Mar is not allowed because the letter *m* is not connected to the letter *a*.
- You may not use the same letter twice in a row *(e.g., meet)*, but you can go back and use a letter again in the same word.
- Plurals are allowed.

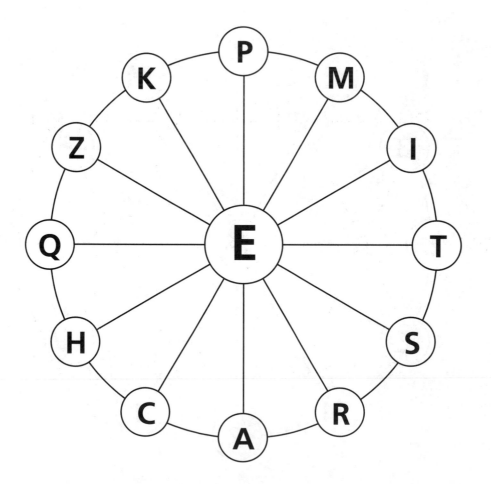

Word Games • 6-8 © 2005 Creative Teaching Press

Zig Zag

VOCABULARY AND SPELLING

How many words can you find in the circles? Write the words you find on a separate sheet of paper.
*Hint: There are more than **60** words.*

Rules
- The words you find must have three or more letters.
- Start on any circle and move to an adjacent circle connected by a line to spell a word.
  You may not skip a circle.

> Examples: *Arm* is allowed because each circle is connected by a line.
>
> *Art* is not allowed because the letter *r* is not connected to the letter *t*.

- You may not use the same letter twice in a row *(e.g., deed)*, but you can go back and
  use a letter again in the same word *(e.g., did)*.
- Plurals are allowed.

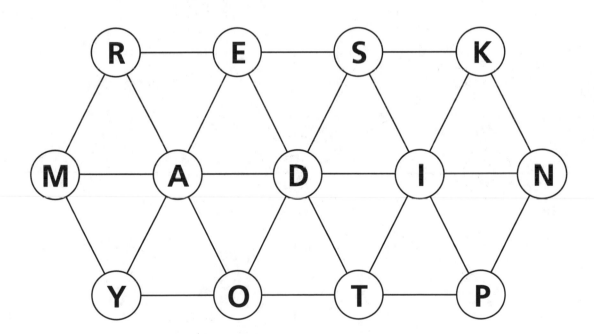

Name _____ Date _____

More Zig Zag
Vocabulary and Spelling

How many words can you find in the circles? Write the words you find on a separate sheet of paper.
*Hint: There are more than **60** words.*

Rules
- The words you find must have three or more letters.
- Start on any circle and move to an adjacent circle connected by a line to spell a word.
  You may not skip a circle.
  > Examples: *King* is allowed because each circle is connected by a line.
  > *Ring* is not allowed because the letter *r* is not connected to the letter *i*.
- You may not use the same letter twice in a row *(e.g., reek)*, but you can go back and use a letter again in the same word *(e.g., tilt)*.

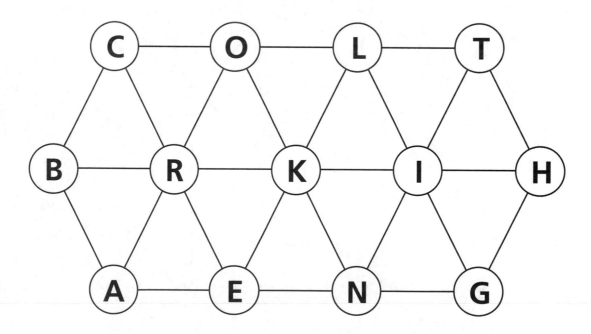

Name _____ Date _____

Star Burst

Vocabulary and Spelling

How many words can you find in the circles? Write the words you find on a separate sheet of paper. *Hint: There are more than 50 words.*

Rules
- The words you find must have three or more letters.
- Start on any circle and move to an adjacent circle connected by a line to spell a word. You may not skip a circle.
  - Examples: *New* is allowed because each circle is connected by a line.
  - *Net* is not allowed because the letter *e* is not connected to the letter *t*.
- You may not use the same letter twice in a row (*e.g., see*), but you can go back and use a letter again in the same word (*e.g., pep*).
- Plurals are allowed.

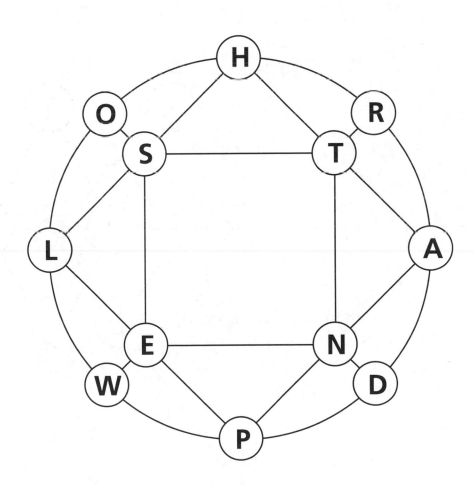

Diamond Puzzle

VOCABULARY AND SPELLING

How many words can you find in the circles? Write the words you find on a separate sheet of paper. *Hint: There are more than **65** words.*

Rules
* The words you find must have three or more letters.
* Start on any circle and move to an adjacent circle connected by a line to spell a word. You may not skip a circle.

    Examples: *Hen* is allowed because each circle is connected by a line.

    Wed is not allowed because the letter *e* is not connected to the letter *d*.
* You may not use the same letter twice in a row *(e.g., add)*, but you can go back and use a letter again in the same word *(e.g., dad)*.
* Plurals are allowed.

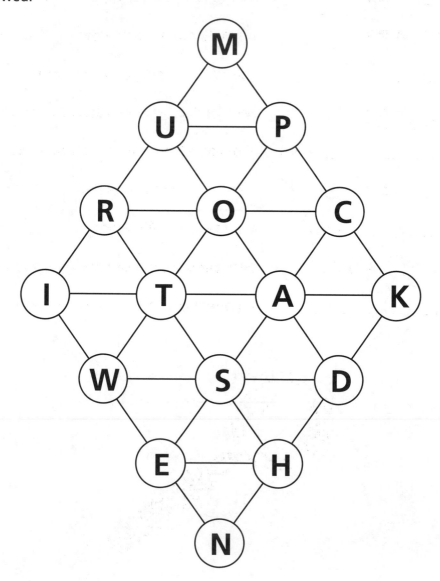

Hidden Ant

VOCABULARY AND SPELLING

Each of the words below has the word *ant* in it. Fill in the missing letters using the definitions on the right as clues. Each line stands for a missing letter.

1 __ __ __ A N T — a pupil who skips school without permission

2 __ A N T __ __ — playful teasing or joking

3 A N T __ __ __ __ __ — a swift, graceful animal with long horns

4 __ __ __ __ A N T — attractive in a dignified or refined way

5 __ __ __ __ A N T — a small, sour berry used for making jellies

6 A N T __ __ __ — the official song of a country

7 __ __ __ __ A N T — remote; far away in space or time

8 __ __ __ __ __ __ __ A N T — a place where meals can be bought and eaten

9 __ __ __ __ A N T __ __ — a promise that something will be done

10 __ __ __ __ __ A N T — very bright; glittering

11 __ __ __ __ __ A N T — very plentiful; more than enough

12 A N T __ __ __ __ __ __ — a collection of poems or stories

Name _____ Date _____

Hidden Art
VOCABULARY AND SPELLING

Each of the words below has the word *art* in it. Fill in the missing letters using the definitions on the right as clues. Each line stands for a missing letter.

1. __ __ A R T — a unit of measure for liquids; two pints

2. A R T __ __ __ __ — any one of the words *a*, *an*, or *the*

3. __ A R T __ __ __ __ — a very small piece

4. __ __ A R T __ __ — frugal; simple

5. A R T __ __ __ __ __ __ — the large group of animals that includes lobsters, insects, spiders, and crabs

6. __ __ __ __ __ __ A R T — one who boasts or talks with too much pride

7. A R T __ __ __ __ __ __ __ — to say in a clear, distinct way

8. __ A R T __ __ __ __ __ — a structure that divides or separates space

9. __ A R T __ __ __ — having to do with war or military life

10. A R T __ __ __ __ __ __ — made by a human being, not by nature

11. __ __ __ __ A R T __ __ __ __ — a part or section of something

12. __ __ __ __ __ __ __ A R T __ __ — a class for five-year-old children

Name _____ Date _____

Hidden Cat

Vocabulary and Spelling

Each of the words below has the word *cat* in it. Fill in the missing letters using the definitions on the right as clues. Each line stands for a missing letter.

1 C A T __ __ __ __ __   a division of a main subject or group; class

2 __ C A T __ __ __   to throw here and there; sprinkle

3 __ __ C A T __   to make a place empty; to leave

4 __ __ C A T __ __ __   the place where something is or will be

5 __ __ __ __ __ C A T __   easily hurt or spoiled; not strong

6 __ __ __ __ __ __ __ C A T __ __   hard to solve, understand, or do

7 __ __ __ __ __ C A T __   to point out; make known

8 C A T __ __ __   cows, bulls, steers, and oxen

9 __ __ __ __ __ __ C A T __   hard to follow or grasp because complicated

10 C A T __ __ __ __ __   something that speeds or provokes change or action

11 __ __ __ __ __ __ C A T __ __ __   something that is not true or has been made up

12 C A T __ __ __ __ __ __ __ __   a terrible disaster

Word Games • 6–8 © 2005 Creative Teaching Press

Name _____ Date _____

Hidden Mat

VOCABULARY AND SPELLING

Each of the words below has the word *mat* in it. Fill in the missing letters using the definitions on the right as clues. Each line stands for a missing letter.

1 M A T __ __ __   what all things are made of; anything that takes up space

2 M A T __ __ __   fully grown

3 __ __ __ M A T __ __ __   arrangement; the way something is put together

4 __ __ __ __ M A T __   final; last

5 M A T __ __ __ __   a concert or a play that takes place in the afternoon

6 __ __ __ __ __ __ M A T   a person in a government whose work is dealing with the government of other nations

7 M A T __ __ __ __ __ __   marriage; the condition of being married

8 __ __ __ M A T __   any member of the most highly developed order of animals such as humans, monkeys, and apes

9 M A T __ __ __ __ __   related to a person on the person's mother's side

10 __ __ __ __ M A T __ __ __ __   of or according to the rules of grammar

Word Games • 6–8 © 2005 Creative Teaching Press

Name _____ Date _____

Hidden Men

VOCABULARY AND SPELLING

Each of the words below has the word *men* in it. Fill in the missing letters using the definitions on the right as clues. Each line stands for a missing letter.

1 M E N __ __ __   a threat or danger

2 M E N __ __ __ __   to speak or write about in just a few words

3 __ __ M E N __ __ __ __   lasting for only a moment

4 __ M E N __ __ __ __ __   a change in or addition to something such as a law

5 M E N __ __ __ __ __ __   someone who begs for money, usually in the street

6 __ __ __ __ M E N __   a written record that is used to prove something

7 __ __ __ __ __ M E N __   a specially shaped tool used for a particular task

8 __ __ __ __ __ __ M E N __   something said when a person wants to praise, approve, or admire

9 __ __ __ __ __ __ __ M E N __   an arrangement to meet someone at a particular place and time

10 __ __ __ __ __ M E N __   an addition or increase in the size of something

11 __ __ __ __ __ __ M E N __   a person or thing that takes the place of another

12 __ __ __ __ __ __ M E N __   something that completes a whole or makes something perfect

Name _____ Date _____

Hidden Pan

Vocabulary and Spelling

Each of the words below has the word *pan* in it. Fill in the missing letters using the definitions on the right as clues. Each line stands for a missing letter.

1 P A N __ __   a sudden, wild fear that is not controlled

2 P A N __ __ __ __   a black leopard

3 __ __ __ P A N __   a group of people joined together in some kind of work or activity

4 P A N __ __ __   a small room near a kitchen where food and dishes are kept

5 __ __ __ P A N __ __ __   a person who goes along with or spends time with another; comrade

6 __ __ P A N __ __   a large, open area

7 P A N __ __ __ __   a large gland behind the stomach

8 P A N __ __ __ __ __   an open view in all directions

9 __ P A N __ __ __   one of the small, shiny pieces of metal sewn on some clothing as a decoration

10 P A N __ __ __ __ __ __ __ __   a wild uproar; chaos

Word Games • 6–8 © 2005 Creative Teaching Press

Name _____ Date _____

Hidden Pen

Vocabulary and Spelling

Each of the words below has the word *pen* in it. Fill in the missing letters using the definitions on the right as clues. Each line stands for a missing letter.

1 P E N __ __ __ __   thinking deeply about something

2 __ __ __ P E N __   a snake; especially a large or poisonous one

3 P E N __ __ __ __   a long, narrow flag or banner, usually in the shape of a triangle

4 __ __ P E N __ __ __   an extra section added to the end of a book that gives more information about the subject in the form of a list, chart, or table

5 P E N __ __ __ __ __ __   a narrow piece of land that juts out from the mainland into a sea or lake

6 __ __ P E N __ __ __ __   having a high price; costing much

7 P E N __ __ __ __ __ __   to pass into or through; pierce

8 P E N __ __ __ __ __   a weight hung so that it swings back and forth

9 __ __ __ __ P E N __ __ __ __   not ruled or controlled by another

10 __ __ __ P E N __ __ __ __   to make up for; take the place of; pay or repay

Word Games • 6–8 © 2005 Creative Teaching Press

Name _____ Date _____

Hidden Rat

Vocabulary and Spelling

Each of the words below has the word *rat* in it. Fill in the missing letters using the definitions on the right as clues. Each line stands for a missing letter.

1 R A T __ __   the relation or comparison of number or size between two different things

2 R A T __ __ __   to approve in an official way

3 __ __ R A T __ __ __   a clever plan or system

4 R A T __ __ __   a fixed share or portion, especially of food

5 __ __ R A T __   to scold somebody vigorously

6 R A T __ __ __   to make or cause to make a series of sharp, short sounds

7 __ __ __ __ __ __ __ R A T __   to say that something is larger or greater than it really is

8 __ __ R A T __ __ __   a race for runners covering a distance of 26 miles, 385 yards

9 __ __ __ __ R A T __   to add something in order to make prettier or more pleasing; to ornament

10 __ __ __ __ __ __ R A T __ __ __   the act or process of recording information in a register or record

Word Games • 6–8 © 2005 Creative Teaching Press

Name _____ Date _____

Hidden Tan

Vocabulary and Spelling

Each of the words below has the word *tan* in it. Fill in the missing letters using the definitions on the right as clues. Each line stands for a missing letter.

1 T A N __ __ __   to make or become knotted or mixed up

2 T A N __ __   having a sharp, strong taste or smell

3 __ T A N __ __ __ __   a level of excellence or quality

4 __ __ __ __ __ T A N __   not changing; staying the same

5 T A N __ __ __ __   a fit of bad temper

6 T A N __ __ __ __ __ __   a small orange with a loose skin and sections that come apart easily

7 __ __ __ __ __ __ T A N __ __   the power to resist or withstand

8 __ __ __ __ __ T A N __ __   approval or belief

9 __ __ __ __ __ T A N __   having much meaning or value

10 __ __ __ __ __ __ __ T A N   a large ape with long arms and shaggy, reddish hair

11 __ __ __ __ __ __ __ __ __ T A N   having to do with a large city and its suburbs

12 T A N __ __ __ __ __ __   to tease or torment

Name _____ Date _____

Hidden Ten

Vocabulary and Spelling

Each of the words below has the word *ten* in it. Fill in the missing letters using the definitions on the right as clues. Each line stands for a missing letter.

1. __ __ T E N __   to be present at

2. T E N __ __ __ __   nervous strain; an anxious feeling

3. __ __ T E N   many times; frequently

4. T E N __ __ __   the cord of tough fiber that fastens a muscle to a bone or other body part

5. __ __ __ T E N __ __   a false claim, excuse, or show

6. T E N __ __ __ __   any one of the small, curling stems that hold up a climbing plant by coiling around something

7. __ __ T E N __ __   very strong or deep; extreme; very great

8. T E N __ __ __ __ __   an old, crowded apartment house in the poorer part of a city

9. __ __ T E N __ __ __ __   capable of coming into being but not yet actual; possible

10. T E N __ __ __ __ __   the fact of being likely to move or act in a certain way

Word Games • 6–8 © 2005 Creative Teaching Press

Name _____ Date _____

Bird Search

SPELLING, VOCABULARY, AND SCIENCE

Find and circle the names of the birds hidden in the puzzle. The names can be found going forward, backward, up, down, and diagonally.

albatross	auk	bobolink	cardinal	cockatoo
condor	cormorant	eagle	egret	falcon
flamingo	grebe	heron	ibis	jackdaw
loon	macaw	mockingbird	myna	oriole
partridge	pelican	penguin	robin	sparrow
thrush	vulture	warbler	whippoorwill	woodpecker

```
S  I  B  I  T  Z  K  S  X  M  W  T  C  E  V
H  E  R  O  N  T  P  T  I  V  H  P  A  X  V
P  Y  L  K  A  A  V  W  L  R  I  C  R  U  S
D  S  U  E  R  U  T  L  U  V  P  O  D  B  G
P  A  S  R  O  S  M  S  O  N  P  M  I  W  P
R  E  O  O  M  G  H  A  E  Z  O  C  N  A  E
E  W  L  B  R  V  N  G  C  C  O  O  A  D  N
L  T  C  I  O  T  D  I  K  A  R  N  L  K  G
B  N  E  N  C  I  A  I  M  E  W  D  A  C  U
R  O  B  R  R  A  N  B  L  A  I  O  N  A  I
A  C  E  T  G  G  N  O  L  E  L  R  Y  J  N
W  L  R  Z  B  E  I  N  H  A  L  F  M  G  B
K  A  G  I  F  R  E  K  C  E  P  D  O  O  W
P  F  R  B  O  B  O  L  I  N  K  M  N  B  C
U  D  O  O  T  A  K  C  O  C  E  L  G  A  E
```

Just for Fun
Do research to learn more about three of the birds listed above. Write five fascinating facts you learned about each bird, and draw a picture of each bird.

Name _____ Date _____

Bone Search

SPELLING, VOCABULARY, AND SCIENCE

Find and circle the names of the bones hidden in the puzzle. The names can be found going forward, backward, up, down, and diagonally.

calcaneus	lumbar vertebrae	radius	carpus	mandible
ribs	clavicle	maxilla	sacrum	coccyx
metacarpus	scapula	femur	metatarsus	sternum
fibula	patella	tarsus	humerus	pelvis
tibia	ilium	phalanges	ulna	ischium
pubis	vertebra			

```
P X V E H X L M M M K S P V E C A
A Y H K L Q T L A E U H X A N A R
T C V R I B S G Y X A I R N M L B
E C I S C H I U M L I B L N S C E
L O H R B M S D A R E L D I A A T
L C G B A C E N T Z S L L C N R
A G X D A D G T R A U S U A R E V
B X I P A E I E A R M B U G U U V
A J U I S H V U E T I O P P M S T
J L B S C R P M S F A F U Q R A L
A I Q I A R U M E F C R B L R A X
T H O B W H M U N R E T S S N O C
L Z M U G E G W A E T E U U U A D
J U T P V R V O H D H S C E S Y R
L O A B O M E T A C A R P U S O Q
P E L V I S R R R C B J Z A Z X W
C X B C V W Z D E L C I V A L C O
```

 Just for Fun
Select eight bones from the puzzle. Tell where each bone is located in the human body.

Word Games • 6–8 © 2005 Creative Teaching Press

Name _____ Date _____

Color Search

Spelling, Vocabulary, and Science

Find and circle the names of the colors hidden in the puzzle. The names can be found going forward, backward, up, down, and diagonally.

alabaster	crimson	magenta	amber	ebony
malachite	auburn	ecru	maroon	azure
emerald	ruby	beige	fuchsia	saffron
carmine	hazel	scarlet	celadon	henna
taupe	chartreuse	indigo	teal	cobalt
khaki	turquoise	coral	lavender	vermilion

```
Y  N  O  B  E  E  E  V  R  A  C  A  T  P  D
O  R  W  E  D  C  C  E  L  G  Z  E  W  L  E
G  F  Y  B  O  X  T  R  Y  E  A  U  A  O  S
I  C  H  R  J  S  T  M  U  L  Z  R  R  Q  U
D  M  A  L  A  C  H  I  T  E  E  A  L  E  E
N  L  T  B  R  T  R  L  M  M  I  A  H  S  R
I  T  A  U  P  E  U  I  E  A  V  V  C  R  T
S  L  B  B  R  W  B  O  T  E  G  A  G  N  R
A  W  E  N  B  Q  Y  N  N  L  R  E  O  X  A
F  A  I  O  Z  C  U  D  O  L  A  O  N  I  H
F  N  G  S  G  V  E  O  E  D  R  B  K  T  C
R  N  E  M  T  R  I  T  I  A  A  A  O  E  A
O  E  N  I  M  R  A  C  M  S  H  L  S  C  Q
N  H  N  R  U  B  U  A  L  K  E  V  E  W  Z
F  U  S  C  H  I  A  M  B  E  R  K  F  C  A
```

 Just for Fun
Make a chart listing the following colors at the top: brown, blue, red, yellow, purple, white, orange, and black. Then place each of the colors in the word search puzzle under the correct heading.

Word Games • 6–8 © 2005 Creative Teaching Press

Flower Search

Spelling, Vocabulary, and Science

Find and circle the names of the flowers hidden in the puzzle. The names can be found going forward, backward, up, down, and diagonally.

anemone	fuchsia	marigold	azalea	gardenia
orchid	begonia	geranium	pansy	buttercup
gladiolus	peony	carnation	heather	petunia
crocus	hibiscus	rhododendron	daffodil	hydrangea
rose	daisy	iris	snapdragon	dandelion
jasmine	tulip	freesia	lilac	violet

```
S  N  P  C  B  R  P  H  P  S  F  K  A  S  T  I  B
U  J  O  E  G  E  H  E  E  J  U  H  V  E  A  U  A
L  A  P  I  T  A  O  O  A  A  I  C  L  L  T  C  I  N
O  S  A  U  L  N  R  E  D  B  T  O  O  T  K  A  I  N
I  M  N  Z  Y  E  G  D  I  O  I  H  E  R  I  D  O  G
D  I  S  G  J  N  D  S  E  V  D  R  E  S  C  I  G  E
A  N  Y  E  A  W  C  N  T  N  C  E  E  R  E  H  G  E
L  E  M  R  L  U  L  A  A  U  I  E  N  A  S  C  B  B
G  F  D  A  S  V  T  P  P  D  R  A  S  D  O  R  E  E
E  Y  L  N  Z  E  C  D  D  F  G  I  C  I  R  O  B  B
H  N  B  I  K  K  R  R  A  E  L  A  Z  A  R  O  U  U
S  F  O  U  L  I  Z  A  X  R  F  Q  G  Y  W  I  N  C
Q  L  Z  M  A  A  L  G  K  E  P  I  L  U  T  N  C
K  R  Q  H  E  O  C  O  I  D  A  I  S  Y  O  Z  I  I
U  F  A  L  V  N  F  N  F  U  C  H  S  I  A  D  E  E
D  L  O  G  I  R  A  M  U  D  A  F  F  O  D  I  L
N  O  I  T  A  N  R  A  C  D  B  N  Q  C  A  B  U
```

 Just for Fun
Draw and color a picture of a garden with at least six of the flowers from the word search puzzle.

Word Games • 6–8 © 2005 Creative Teaching Press

Name _____ Date _____

Health and Nutrition Search

SPELLING, VOCABULARY, AND SCIENCE

Find and circle the health and nutrition words hidden in the puzzle. The words can be found going forward, backward, up, down, and diagonally.

absorption	fiber	phosphorus	amino acids	fruits
potassium	calcium	glucose	proteins	calorie
grains	salts	carbohydrate	iron	starches
cereals	metabolism	stomach	cholesterol	minerals
sugars	energy	nutrients	vegetables	enzyme
nutrition	vitamins	fats	pancreas	water

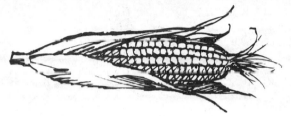

```
M  D  C  L  I  M  U  D  L  E  P  L  P  T  C  S  V
U  N  O  I  T  I  R  T  U  N  N  Q  M  A  K  D  E
I  S  E  R  C  N  Q  O  S  M  V  E  R  Y  V  I  G
S  L  N  E  F  W  O  L  S  N  E  B  R  I  O  C  E
S  A  Z  B  L  P  A  I  U  E  O  W  T  G  E  A  T
A  E  Y  I  X  R  L  T  T  H  I  A  P  S  Y  O  A
T  R  M  F  E  O  R  F  Y  P  M  R  O  Y  T  N  B
O  E  E  N  B  I  R  D  S  I  R  C  O  Z  X  I  L
P  C  I  A  E  U  R  Z  N  R  U  O  C  L  V  M  E
U  M  T  N  I  A  W  S  P  L  A  T  S  C  A  A  S
L  E  T  T  T  W  H  D  G  R  O  G  F  B  F  C  T
M  S  S  E  P  H  O  S  P  H  O  R  U  S  A  S  A
P  W  N  E  M  U  I  C  L  A  C  T  L  S  T  I  R
K  Y  S  T  O  M  A  C  H  V  F  U  E  L  O  R  C
W  A  T  E  R  S  N  I  A  R  G  A  A  I  E  O  H
L  O  R  E  T  S  E  L  O  H  C  S  T  Q  N  N  E
P  A  N  C  R  E  A  S  L  U  C  Y  H  S  E  S  S
```

Just for Fun
Make a word search puzzle for a friend to solve using the names of 30 things to eat. Include foods from each of the food groups. Make an answer key for your puzzle.

Mammal Search

Spelling, Vocabulary, and Science

Find and circle the names of the mammals hidden in the puzzle. The names can be found going forward, backward, up, down, and diagonally.

aardvark	armadillo	baboon	badger	beaver
capybara	chimpanzee	coati	coyote	eland
gnu	hippopotamus	ibex	jackal	jaguar
kinkajou	lemur	llama	ocelot	okapi
opossum	orangutan	porcupine	rhinoceros	skunk
sloth	tapir	warthog	yak	zebu

```
O  L  L  A  M  A  M  O  T  E  N  K  D  R  G  S  H
F  L  U  P  Q  N  P  N  N  R  A  I  N  E  Z  K  I
T  O  L  E  C  O  B  I  R  J  T  N  A  G  E  U  P
W  N  S  I  S  D  P  T  A  E  U  K  L  D  P  N  P
J  B  O  S  D  U  L  G  E  X  G  A  E  A  N  K  O
A  C  U  O  C  A  U  Y  A  K  N  J  F  B  S  V  P
C  M  A  R  B  A  M  M  M  C  A  O  X  V  B  C  O
K  O  O  P  R  A  R  R  H  X  R  U  F  Z  K  A  T
A  P  K  U  Y  E  B  I  A  G  O  H  T  R  A  W  A
L  X  M  A  V  B  M  A  A  R  D  V  A  R  K  V  M
E  E  E  A  P  P  A  C  O  Y  O  T  E  V  C  E  U
L  W  E  B  A  I  U  R  A  G  I  R  I  P  A  T  S
Y  B  N  N  I  N  Q  N  A  F  I  T  O  A  C  S  U
Q  D  Z  C  G  U  D  M  A  M  E  B  A  O  L  Z  B
F  E  S  O  R  E  C  O  N  I  H  R  B  O  J  X  E
E  G  P  W  A  U  Z  I  D  W  I  N  T  K  C  T  Z
S  G  S  R  Y  V  I  Z  P  C  D  H  A  F  Y  N  A
```

Just for Fun
Select the names of six mammals from the puzzle. Do research to learn five fascinating facts about each one.

Word Games • 6–8 © 2005 Creative Teaching Press

Name _____ Date _____

Solar System Search

SPELLING, VOCABULARY, AND SCIENCE

Find and circle the solar system words hidden in the puzzle. The words can be found going forward, backward, up, down, and diagonally.

apex	apogee	asteroid	astronomy	aurora
axis	black hole	chromosphere	comet	constellation
corona	craters	dwarf	eclipse	ellipse
equinox	galaxy	light-year	lunar	magnitude
meteor	meteorite	nebula	penumbra	planet
satellite	sunspots	supernova	umbra	zenith

```
S  U  P  E  R  N  O  V  A  N  K  A  C  L  E  P  C
I  R  O  E  T  E  M  X  E  P  A  S  O  U  M  E  O
R  A  E  Y  T  H  G  I  L  E  L  T  R  N  D  N  Z
C  O  M  E  T  A  D  C  W  U  U  R  O  A  I  U  X
C  O  N  S  T  E  L  L  A  T  I  O  N  R  N  M  T
E  H  M  Q  U  D  E  U  C  L  V  N  A  N  E  B  E
C  S  R  M  N  H  W  D  B  I  I  O  J  W  T  R  N
M  P  B  O  T  R  G  A  U  E  E  M  T  B  I  A  A
Q  R  A  I  M  A  Y  S  R  T  N  Y  L  X  R  E  L
A  L  N  S  L  O  U  I  I  F  I  A  O  R  O  S  P
W  E  E  A  T  N  S  L  A  Y  C  N  T  V  E  P  S
Z  M  X  S  S  E  L  P  U  K  I  A  G  G  T  I  C
S  Y  O  P  P  E  R  A  H  U  M  Z  U  A  E  L  M
X  I  O  D  T  I  G  O  Q  E  B  H  T  R  M  L  F
W  T  X  A  V  M  L  E  I  F  R  Q  O  H  O  E  D
S  B  S  A  U  E  F  C  S  D  Q  E  I  Y  P  R  Y
S  R  E  T  A  R  C  V  E  A  P  O  G  E  E  S  A
```

Just for Fun
Write and illustrate a story about an extraterrestrial visitor.

Name _____   Date _____

 # Weather Search
SPELLING, VOCABULARY, AND SCIENCE

Find and circle the weather words hidden in the puzzle. The names can be found going forward, backward, up, down, and diagonally.

altocumulus	blizzard	cirrus	cloud	cumulus
cyclone	dew	drizzle	fog	frost
hailstone	humidity	hurricane	icicle	lightning
mist	monsoon	nimbostratus	precipitation	rain
sleet	smog	snowstorm	squall	stratocumulus
temperature	thunderbolt	tornado	typhoon	windstorm

```
I A K B S E C U O D S G S O G H I T
E H L W L U L D W Q T U R W N U C E
H N I T M I A Z U U L L C M I M I E
C Q A U O N Z A Z U B T N D N I C L
X I L C R C L Z M I H F O T T D L S
T U R O I L U U A U R M I E H I E F
S S T R I R C M N R R D T M G T U T
P G O V U O R D U O D E A P I Y S P
E R O R T S E U T L Y W T E L I B N
O L B A F R D S H E U I I R M L C A
T L R K B L W R A I N S P A W P N Y
B T P O Q O D V J J B A I T I C O J
S S L E N O L C Y C I A C U C K O A
A T B S T Y P H O O N V E R S F S D
N I M B O S T R A T U S R E O M N T
E N O T S L I A H Y G B P G V M O R
D U O L C S H Z W I N D S T O R M G
Q P O X B B F X I Z N Y S P R W B L
```

  Just for Fun
Do research to learn more about three of the weather words listed above. Write five fascinating facts you learned about each bird, and draw a picture of each bird.

Word Games • 6–8 © 2005 Creative Teaching Press

Name _____ Date _____

Capital Search

Spelling, Vocabulary, and Social Studies

Find and circle the United States capitals hidden in the puzzle. The names of the capitals can be found going forward, backward, up, down, and diagonally.

Augusta	Bismarck	Boise	Boston	Cheyenne
Concord	Des Moines	Dover	Frankfort	Harrisburg
Hartford	Honolulu	Indianapolis	Juneau	Lansing
Madison	Montgomery	Montpelier	Olympia	Pierre
Providence	Raleigh	Richmond	Sacramento	Salem
Santa Fe	Springfield	Tallahassee	Topeka	Trenton

```
F  R  M  C  U  S  Z  X  G  H  L  T  G  H  E  B  U
E  R  Z  B  A  A  S  R  K  J  H  A  H  Q  C  I  L
R  P  A  D  O  P  E  L  R  H  C  L  G  D  N  S  U
Z  F  I  N  D  I  A  N  A  P  O  L  I  S  E  M  L
A  C  I  O  K  N  S  R  U  T  N  A  E  T  D  A  O
J  I  V  L  S  F  R  E  N  J  C  H  L  R  I  R  N
S  E  P  I  E  I  O  E  Q  H  O  A  A  E  V  C  O
R  P  N  M  S  P  M  R  E  U  R  S  R  N  O  K  H
A  G  R  B  Y  A  T  Y  T  R  D  S  S  T  R  N  E
R  U  U  I  R  L  E  N  A  H  I  E  T  O  P  I  R
Y  R  G  C  N  N  O  Y  O  S  M  E  R  N  K  C  R
G  B  A  U  N  G  Y  R  E  M  O  G  T  N  O  M  E
P  S  Z  E  S  I  F  L  D  R  O  F  T  R  A  H  I
M  E  L  A  S  T  R  I  C  H  M  O  N  D  R  L  P
H  N  O  S  I  D  A  M  E  S  A  N  T  A  F  E  U
D  E  S  M  O  I  N  E  S  L  N  O  T  S  O  B  A
T  O  P  E  K  A  K  K  P  M  D  P  K  D  P  K  Z
```

Just for Fun
Make a list of the 20 state capitals that are not in the puzzle. Make a word search puzzle with these names for a classmate to solve. Make an answer key for your puzzle.

Name _____   Date _____

Nations of Africa Search

WORLD GEOGRAPHY

Find and circle the names of the African nations that are hidden in the puzzle. The names can be found going forward, backward, up, down, and diagonally.

Algeria	Angola	Botswana	Cameroon	Chad
Egypt	Gabon	Ghana	Guinea	Kenya
Lesotho	Liberia	Madagascar	Malawi	Mali
Mauritania	Morocco	Mozambique	Namibia	Rwanda
Senegal	Sierra Leone	Somalia	South Africa	Sudan
Swaziland	Tanzania	Uganda	Zambia	Zimbabwe

```
D C D E U C Z O I S F A L O Z X Z
A H B U G G A W H I Z J C V A I B
G A U Q W Z A M D E J C S L M V M
A D E I G L G N E R O O D B B O D
I I J B A R A Q D R M S A D I Z S
R C N M O L R J O A O B U O A O S
E D L A I H C M L L W O Z D U A W
B A N Z T V T I J E O A N T A E S
I C A O M I A O P O Z T H F N N E
L W I M W Z R B S N K A Z Z A I N
S A L O G N A U J E F N N X H U E
B O T S W A N A A R L Z G O G G G
V R W A N D A A I M N A M I B I A
K E N Y A M O C T E U N I R G A L
R A C S A G A D A M H I O U L O G
N L W L Z T K N Z H O A U B M V Q
T Y I A I R E G L A T P Y G E D V
```

Just for Fun
Using the resources of your school library or the Internet, find three recipes for African foods. Share your findings with your classmates.

Word Games • 6–8 © 2005 Creative Teaching Press

Nations of Asia Search

WORLD GEOGRAPHY

Find and circle the names of the Asian nations that are hidden in the puzzle. The names can be found going forward, backward, up, down, and diagonally.

Afghanistan	Armenia	Azerbaijan	Bahrain	Bangladesh
Belarus	Bhutan	Bosnia	Brunei	Cambodia
China	Cyprus	Estonia	Georgia	Herzegovina
India	Indonesia	Iran	Iraq	Israel
Japan	Jordan	Kazakhstan	Kiribati	Kuwait
Kyrgyzstan	Laos	Lebanon	North Korea	South Korea

```
N H C Q N K I K I B C A B E I L A
A E A A A A M L Z N Z T H J I E M
T R M Q F R T H S E D A L G N A B
S Z B L R G I S R U E O I M D R I
Z E O B E C H B H R R K N B I S B
Y G D H P B A A O K I P O E A I S
G O I U I I A K N R A S Y C S Y U
R V A T J N H N I I N Z G C O I R
Y I O A N T H B O I S I A P A W A
K N N N R C A O A N P T A K L A L
Q A S O U T H K O R E A A R I U E
U X N V I H A I N E M R A N H O B
G E O R G I A A N D J V O E C A T
I E N U R B D P W A Z T N A R I B
P R T C A R J I P Y S K U W A I T
C N W K O S X A J E I Y O P F T X
K J Y J V I N X L Y K R P L F P B
```

Just for Fun
Use the resources of your school library or the Internet to draw the flags of six or more of these Asian nations.

Nations of Europe Search

WORLD GEOGRAPHY

Find and circle the names of the European nations that are hidden in the puzzle. The names can be found going forward, backward, up, down, and diagonally.

Albania	Andorra	Austria	Belgium	Bulgaria
Croatia	Denmark	Finland	France	Germany
Greece	Hungary	Ireland	Italy	Latvia
Lithuania	Luxembourg	Macedonia	Malta	Moldova
Monaco	Netherlands	Norway	Poland	Portugal
Romania	Slovakia	Spain	Switzerland	United Kingdom

```
A N D O R R A F M J S A L Z B P I
L M A O D F A A E D Q I I I E O N
D F P U R N C T N C O K T R L L I
Y U Z A S E A A L C C A H U G A A
C Q N L D T L L A A L V U M I N P
L C N O A R R N N Y M O A O U D S
E U N O E G O I P I G L N D M Y Z
M I X H R M U A A J F S I G M N M
A O T E S W I T Z E R L A N D A R
W E L L M N A C R Y E J U I L M O
N G K D A B R Y R O Q C I K R R M
A C O B O O O A P A P Q E D Y E A
I Q L O A V G U K R A M N E D G N
V A X T Y N A K R A I N D T R O I
T V I U U D M Q G G L T R I E G A
A A X H I R E L A N D Z M N S T T
L S N A A I R A G L U B T U I G L
```

Just for Fun

Choose eight or more countries from the list that are not familiar to you. Using the resources of your school library or the Internet, list the country and the type of government it has.

Word Games • 6–8 © 2005 Creative Teaching Press

Occupation Search

SPELLING, VOCABULARY, AND SOCIAL STUDIES

Find and circle the occupation words hidden in the puzzle. Words can be found going forward, backward, up, down, and diagonally.

accountant	archaeologist	artist	banker	biologist
carpenter	electrician	farmer	firefighter	inventor
investigator	janitor	journalist	librarian	mechanic
meteorologist	nurse	painter	paramedic	photographer
plumber	politician	realtor	sculptor	social worker
teacher	travel agent	truck driver	veterinarian	welder

```
T  C  R  E  B  R  X  U  L  B  E  R  A  R  B  T  C  C  P
M  S  I  R  F  I  P  F  N  C  E  T  U  O  S  N  A  I  A
T  S  I  G  O  L  O  E  A  H  C  R  A  T  D  A  R  N  I
Y  V  J  G  U  T  N  L  P  R  F  U  S  A  E  T  P  A  N
R  A  E  M  O  U  N  A  O  I  M  I  R  G  L  N  E  H  T
N  E  B  T  R  L  R  E  R  G  L  E  L  I  E  U  N  C  E
J  E  V  S  E  G  O  E  V  A  I  I  R  T  C  O  T  E  R
R  A  E  I  O  R  F  R  N  N  B  S  S  S  T  C  E  M  E
B  T  N  T  R  I  I  R  O  R  I  I  T  E  R  C  R  W  H
S  Z  O  I  G  D  U  N  A  E  T  Z  H  V  I  A  E  E  C
G  H  G  H  T  O  K  R  A  R  T  H  A  N  C  Q  Y  L  A
P  D  T  H  J  O  I  C  A  R  V  E  Q  I  I  K  L  D  E
P  E  X  F  P  A  R  P  U  O  I  M  M  H  A  L  R  E  T
R  S  B  A  N  K  E  R  F  R  Y  A  J  Z  N  M  Y  R  F
P  O  L  I  T  I  C  I  A  N  T  E  N  Z  V  U  E  Z  T
R  O  T  L  A  E  R  S  O  C  I  A  L  W  O  R  K  E  R
G  T  N  E  G  A  L  E  V  A  R  T  Z  C  C  P  I  I  T
S  C  U  L  P  T  O  R  C  I  D  E  M  A  R  A  P  R  B
O  G  Y  L  D  O  B  B  T  S  Z  O  Q  C  E  B  V  M  G
```

Just for Fun
Choose an occupation from the list, and write a short story about a special or unusual day in the life of that person.

Word Games • 6–8 © 2005 Creative Teaching Press

President Search

SOCIAL STUDIES

Find and circle the last names of United States presidents hidden in the puzzle. The names can be found going forward, backward, up, down, and diagonally.

Adams	Buchanan	Bush	Carter	Cleveland
Clinton	Coolidge	Eisenhower	Ford	Garfield
Grant	Harding	Harrison	Hayes	Kennedy
Jackson	Jefferson	Johnson	Lincoln	Madison
Monroe	Nixon	Polk	Reagan	Roosevelt
Taylor	Truman	Tyler	Washington	Wilson

```
R N N R T N I N S H N H N K S
O O J E A I J I O O A O S M Q
O S A W Y X Q E T S T Y A U E
S I C O L O D G F N I D E R B
E R K H O N N L I F A D T S X
V R S N R I C L E V E L A N D
E A O E H Y C E J I B R H M R
L H N S P C E O D U F M S E O
T K A I H O H E C T H R E O F
R W E E R N X H R E A G A N N
E P S N S H A R D I N G J G O
T L O O N N E G D I L O O C S
R M N L A E N L O C N I L U L
A D A N K B D N A M U R T W I
C G R A N T W Y R E L Y T D W
```

Just for Fun
Make a list of all the presidents who are not in the puzzle. Make a word search puzzle using these names for a classmate to solve. Make an answer key for your puzzle.

Name _____ Date _____

State Search

GEOGRAPHY

Find and circle the names of the states hidden in the puzzle. The names can be found going forward, backward, up, down, and diagonally.

Alabama	Alaska	Arizona	Arkansas	Colorado
Delaware	Florida	Hawaii	Idaho	Illinois
Indiana	Iowa	Kansas	Kentucky	Maine
Massachusetts	Minnesota	Nebraska	New Mexico	North Carolina
Oklahoma	Oregon	Pennsylvania	Texas	Utah
Vermont	Virginia	Washington	West Virginia	Wyoming

```
M N C V I R G I N I A O T N A T
U A O O I A I E L E J A I O R Y
A T S T L P L L N S O D E R I W
L K A S G O I A O I A D P T Z A
A N S H A N R C B H A E D H O M
S N Q A O C I A O A N M E C N O
K N A I R X H H D N M S L A A H
A I S I E B T U S O W A A R A A
F F M M D N E Y S A S X W O T L
U L W I O N L N Y E W E A L O K
H E W M P V I R K K T T R I S O
N A R K A N S A S J L T E N E R
F E D N Y K C U T N E K S A N E
V A I N I G R I V T S E W X N G
U A P K A D I R O L F O A S I O
I I A W A H W Y O M I N G I M N
```

Just for Fun

Make a list of all the states that are not in the puzzle. Make a word search puzzle using these names for a classmate to solve. Make an answer key for your puzzle.

Name _____ Date _____

Things That Travel on Water Search

SPELLING, VOCABULARY, AND SOCIAL STUDIES

Find and circle the names of things that travel on water hidden in the puzzle. The names can be found going forward, backward, up, down, and diagonally.

barge	brig	canoe	caravel	catamaran
clipper	cruiser	cutter	destroyer	dinghy
dugout	ferryboat	frigate	galleon	gondola
houseboat	hovercraft	hydroplane	kayak	outrigger
pontoon	raft	rowboat	sailboat	sampan
schooner	sloop	steamship	tugboat	yacht

```
T  G  G  L  R  A  K  E  S  T  F  P  Q  R  S  G
A  C  E  M  L  A  C  C  F  E  O  R  S  E  A  O
O  L  C  H  Y  E  H  A  R  N  M  C  D  S  I  N
B  D  H  A  K  O  R  R  T  E  X  K  X  I  L  D
G  E  K  Q  O  C  Y  O  E  A  P  A  B  U  B  O
U  S  G  N  R  B  O  V  E  G  M  P  J  R  O  L
T  T  E  E  O  N  T  F  A  R  R  A  I  C  A  A
Z  R  V  A  G  A  L  L  E  O  N  A  R  L  T  R
T  O  T  A  O  B  E  S  U  O  H  B  B  A  C  E
H  Y  B  G  H  Y  D  R  O  P  L  A  N  E  N  G
H  E  S  T  E  A  M  S  H  I  P  R  T  D  E  G
V  R  T  A  O  B  W  O  R  D  E  A  Y  U  O  I
D  I  N  G  H  Y  H  T  F  T  G  B  A  G  N  R
N  A  P  M  A  S  W  P  T  I  R  N  C  O  A  T
L  E  V  A  R  A  C  U  R  I  W  Y  H  U  C  U
S  L  O  O  P  L  C  F  G  Y  U  X  T  T  N  O
```

 Just for Fun
Select four words from the puzzle, and do research to learn more about each type of water transportation. Draw a picture of each mode of transportation. Label each picture.

Pick a Word

For each category, write words that begin with the letter on the left. Score one point for each correct answer. Earn five bonus points for any category where you have no incorrect answers or blanks. Use a dictionary if you need help finding a word for any category.

Letter	a hyphenated word	a word with a prefix	a word ending in –ing	a pair of homophones	a word with two of the same vowels together	a word with two of the same consonants together	Score
D							
O							
M							
P							
R							
W							
						Total	
						Bonus	
						Final Score	

Suffixes

For each category, write words that begin with the letter on the left. Score one point for each correct answer. Earn five bonus points for any category where you have no incorrect answers or blanks. Use a dictionary if you need help finding a word for any category.

Letter	-able	-ion	-ish	-logy	-ment	-some	Score
B							
C							
F							
L							
M							
T							
						Total	
						Bonus	
						Final Score	

Word Games • 6–8 © 2005 Creative Teaching Press

Syllable Count

For each category, write words that begin with the letter on the left. Score one point for each correct answer. Earn five bonus points for any category where you have no incorrect answers or blanks. Use a dictionary if you need help finding a word for any category.

Letter	words with one syllable	words with two syllables (accent on the 1st syllable)	words with two syllables (accent on the 2nd syllable)	words with three syllables (accent on the 1st syllable)	words with four syllables	words with five syllables	Score
A							
G							
N							
P							
R							
S							
						Total	
						Bonus	
						Final Score	

Parts of Speech

For each category, write words that begin with the letter on the left. Score one point for each correct answer. Earn five bonus points for any category where you have no incorrect answers or blanks. Use a dictionary if you need help finding a word for any category.

Letter	adjective	adverb	noun	preposition	pronoun	verb	Score
E							
M							
N							
O							
T							
Y							
						Total	
						Bonus	
						Final Score	

Geography

For each category, write a word that begins with the letter on the left. Score one point for each correct answer. Earn five bonus points for any category where you have no incorrect answers cr blanks. Use maps, globes, atlases, encyclopedias, and other reference materials if you need help finding a word in any category.

Letter	body of water (river, lake)	city	country	island	mountain	state	Score
A							
C							
I							
N							
S							
W							
						Total	
						Bonus	
						Final Score	

People

For each category, write a word that begins with the letter on the left. Use last names only for each person. You may not use the same person more than once. Score one point for each correct answer. Earn five bonus points for any category where there are no incorrect answers or blanks. Use books, encyclopedias, and other reference materials if you need help finding a word in any category.

Letter	author	explorer	inventor	famous man in history	U.S. president	famous woman in history	Score
B							
E							
F							
H							
K							
R							
						Total	
						Bonus	
						Final Score	

Living Things

For each category, write a word that begins with the letter on the left. Score one point for each correct answer. Earn five bonus points for any category where there are no incorrect answers or blanks. Use books, encyclopedias, and other reference materials if you need help finding a word in any category.

Letter	bird	fish	flower	insect	mammal	tree	Score
C							
O							
P							
R							
T							
W							
						Total	
						Bonus	
						Final Score	

Name _____

Date _____

Foods

For each category, write a word that begins with the letter on the left. Score one point for each correct answer. Earn five bonus points for any category where there are no incorrect answers or blanks. Use books, encyclopedias, and other reference materials if you need help finding a word in any category.

Letter	dessert	fruit	ice cream flavor	main course	sandwich	vegetable	Score
B							
C							
E							
P							
S							
T							
						Total	
						Bonus	
						Final Score	

Word Games • *6–8* © 2005 Creative Teaching Press

Name _____   Date _____

Shopping Spree

For each category, write a word of something you would buy at that store and that begins with the letter on the left. Score one point for each correct answer. Earn five bonus points for any category where there are no incorrect answers or blanks.

Letter	Department Store	Grocery Store	Hardware Store	Office Supply Store	Sporting Goods Store	Toy Store	Score
F							
G							
H							
J							
L							
S							
						Total	
						Bonus	
						Final Score	

Word Games • 6–8 © 2005 Creative Teaching Press

Name _____

Date _____

Odds and Ends

For each category, write a word that begins with the letter on the left. If the book or movie title starts with a, an or the, you may skip that word. Score one point for each correct answer. Earn five bonus points for any category where there are no incorrect answers or blanks.

Letter	book title	a color	a drink	movie title	something round	type of transportation	Score
B							
H							
P							
S							
T							
W							
						Total	
						Bonus	
						Final Score	

Synonym Puzzle

SYNONYMS, VOCABULARY, AND SPELLING

A **synonym** is a word that means the same, or almost the same, as another word such as *false* and *untrue*. Write a synonym for each word to complete the crossword puzzle. Use the words in the box if you need help.

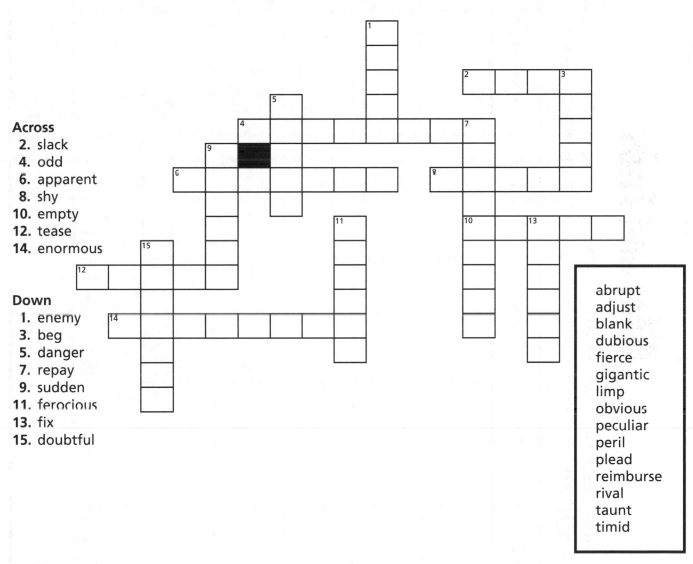

Across
2. slack
4. odd
6. apparent
8. shy
10. empty
12. tease
14. enormous

Down
1. enemy
3. beg
5. danger
7. repay
9. sudden
11. ferocious
13. fix
15. doubtful

abrupt
adjust
blank
dubious
fierce
gigantic
limp
obvious
peculiar
peril
plead
reimburse
rival
taunt
timid

Just for Fun
Write a synonym for each of these words.

a. marvelous _____

b. divulge _____

c. merit _____

d. essential _____

e. tranquil _____

Antonym Puzzle

Synonyms, Vocabulary, and Spelling

An **antonym** is a word that means the opposite of another word. For example, *dark* is an antonym of *light*. Write an antonym for each word to complete the crossword puzzle. Use the words in the box if you need help.

Across
2. temporary
4. polite
6. sturdy
8. complex
10. beneficial
12. deep

Down
1. scarce
3. comply
5. superior
7. minimum
9. busy
11. omit
13. forbid
14. solid
15. exact

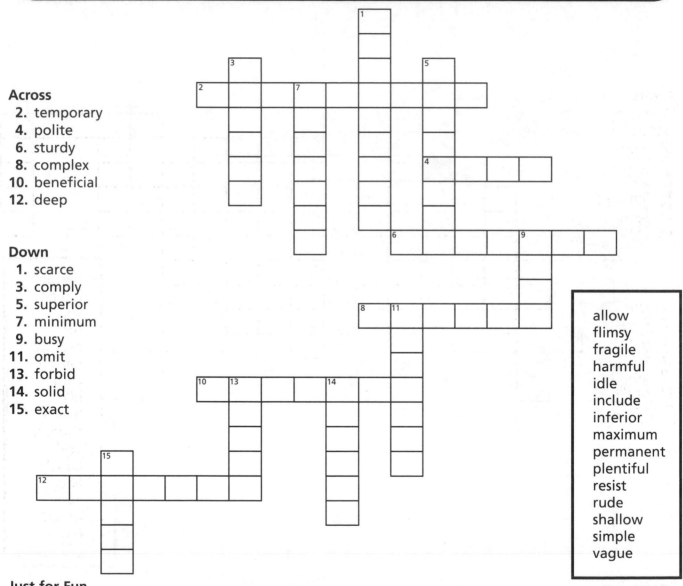

allow
flimsy
fragile
harmful
idle
include
inferior
maximum
permanent
plentiful
resist
rude
shallow
simple
vague

Just for Fun
Write a antonym for each of these words.

a. offense _____

b. nadir _____

c. victory _____

d. somber _____

e. ambitious _____

Word Games • 6-8 © 2005 Creative Teaching Press

Name _____ Date _____

Homophone Puzzle

HOMOPHONES, VOCABULARY, AND SPELLING

Homophones are words that sound alike but have different spellings and meanings, such as *ant* and *aunt*. Write a homophone for each word to complete the crossword puzzle. Use the words in the box if you need help.

Across
2. plum
4. idol
6. yoke
8. oracle
10. air
12. allowed
14. baron
15. aisle

Down
1. lynx
3. beach
5. duel
7. council
9. gourd
11. bridle
13. claws

barren
plumb
yolk
isle
heir
barren
aloud
idle
beech
counsel
bridal
auricle
links
dual
gored
clause

Just for Fun
Write a homophone for each of these words.

a. jeans _____

b. phrase _____

c. maze _____

d. load _____

e. naval _____

Word Games • 6–8 © 2005 Creative Teaching Press

Name _____ Date _____

Noun Puzzle

Synonyms, Vocabulary, and Spelling

> A **noun** is the name of a person, place, thing, quality, or idea. Write the noun that best matches each definition to complete the crossword puzzle. Use the words in the box if you need help.

Across

2. a natural skill; talent
4. a strong liking or interest
6. a large fleet of warships
8. a long, serious poem that tells a story of a hero
10. a general idea
12. the height of a person
14. a small, flat seed that grows in a pod
15. a light, warming breeze

Down

1. a belief that guides a person
3. something that is believed to be true
5. the roof of the mouth
7. something that happens in real life or in a story
9. a tall stone pillar with a pointed top
11. an official order or decision
13. a sign or symbol

armada	assumption	creed
decree	enthusiasm	epic
flair	incident	lentil
notion	obelisk	palate
stature	token	zephyr

Just for Fun

Write the definitions of these nouns.

a. knoll _____

b. tassel _____

c. compulsion _____

d. khaki _____

e. foliage _____

Word Games • 6–8 • © 2005 Creative Teaching Press

Plural Puzzle

Nouns, Plurals, and Spelling

A **noun** is the name of a person, place, thing, quality, or idea. A noun that is **singular** names only one person, place, thing, quality, or idea. A noun that is **plural** names more than one. Write the plural form of each singular noun to complete the crossword puzzle.

Across
2. ox
4. deer
6. octopus
8. wharf
10. sky
12. foot
14. calf
15. soprano

Down
1. moose
3. tax
5. ratio
7. guess
9. daisy
11. studio
13. salmon

Just for Fun
Write the plurals of the following singular nouns.

a. woman _____

b. chimney _____

c. corps _____

d. datum _____

e. larva _____

Word Games • 6–8 © 2005 Creative Teaching Press

Name _____ Date _____

Adjective Puzzle
ADJECTIVES, VOCABULARY, AND SPELLING

An **adjective** is a word that describes a noun or pronoun. An adjective tells how many, what kind, or which one. Write an adjective that matches each description to complete the crossword puzzle. Use the words in the box if you need help.

Across
2. not certain; vague
4. very excited or upset; wild
6. easy to annoy or make angry
8. skillful; quick but sure
10. not real; imaginary
12. short and to the point
13. very cruel; brutal
14. not wanting to do something

Down
1. very odd
3. joyful and proud; glad
5. modest; not proud
6. powerful
7. on or to one side
9. spotless; perfectly clean
11. hot and damp; without a breeze

askew
hazy
jubilant
bizarre
humble
reluctant
concise
immaculate
savage
deft
influential
sultry
fanciful
irritable
turbulent

Just for Fun
Write the definitions of these adjectives.

a. successive _____

b. poky _____

c. hideous _____

d. explicit _____

e. clammy _____

Word Games • 6–8 © 2005 Creative Teaching Press

Name _____ Date _____

Verb Puzzle

VERBS, VOCABULARY, AND SPELLING

A **verb** is a word that expresses an act, an occurrence, or a state of being. Write the verb that matches each definition to complete the crossword puzzle. Use the words in the box if you need help.

Across
2. tell what has happened
4. to wet completely; soak
6. to collect
8. to do away with; cancel
10. to flow out with force and in large amounts; spout
12. to move ahead with difficulty
14. to become less active or intense
15. to stay or wait very close by

Down
1. to cover completely; swallow up
3. to move even a little
5. to make unable to move or act because of fear
7. to cry loudly
9. to walk in an unsteady way
11. to annoy again and again by shouting insults
13. to go, put, or stay underwater

assemble
bawl
budge
drench
engulf
forge
gush
heckle
hover
narrate
petrify
repeal
stagger
submerge
subside

Just for Fun
Write the definitions of these verbs.

a. heed _____

b. consent _____

c. query _____

d. verify _____

e. fidget _____

Name _____ Date _____

Past Participle Puzzle

Verb Tenses, Vocabulary, and Spelling

The **past participle** of a verb shows that the verb's action took place in the past. For example, the past participle of the verb *see* (I <u>see</u> her each day) is *seen* (I <u>have seen</u> her before). The helping verbs *has* or *have* are always used with the past participle. Write the past participle for each verb to complete the crossword puzzle.

Across
2. draw
4. go
6. freeze
8. shrink
10. take
12. see
14. write

Down
1. ride
3. sing
5. spring
7. wear
9. eat
11. shake
13. fly
15. know

Just for Fun
Write the past participle of each of these verbs.

a. come _____

b. hide _____

c. ring _____

d. rise _____

e. run _____

Word Games • 6–8 © 2005 Creative Teaching Press

Name _____ Date _____

Abbreviation Puzzle

ABBREVIATIONS, MEASUREMENT, AND SPELLING

An **abbreviation** is a shortened or contracted form of a word or phrase such as *adj.* for *adjective* or *inc.* for *incorporated*. Write out the word for each abbreviation to complete the crossword puzzle.

Across
2. Ave.
4. Lt.
6. yd.
8. Sept.
10. tsp.
12. Jr.

Down
1. Tues.
3. dept.
5. Blvd.
7. Gov.
9. Thurs.
11. pd.
13. tbsp.
14. Pkwy.
15. corp.

Just for Fun
Write abbreviations for the following words.

a. superintendent _____

b. miscellaneous _____

c. association _____

d. colonel _____

e. elementary _____

State Capitals Puzzle

STATE CAPITALS

Write the name of the capital for each state to complete the crossword puzzle. Use the words in the box if you need help.

Across
2. New Hampshire
4. California
6. Georgia
8. Massachusetts
10. South Dakota
12. Kansas
14. Ohio
15. Illinois

Down
1. Delaware
3. Idaho
5. Connecticut
7. Tennessee
9. Texas
11. Arizona
13. Oregon

Atlanta	Austin	Boise
Boston	Columbus	Concord
Dover	Hartford	Nashville
Phoenix	Pierre	Sacramento
Salem	Springfield	Topeka

Just for Fun
Write the names of the capitals of these states.

a. Arkansas _____

b. North Dakota _____

c. Wyoming _____

d. Montana _____

e. Wisconsin _____

Word Games • 6–8 © 2005 Creative Teaching Press

Animal Offspring Puzzle

SCIENCE, VOCABULARY, AND SPELLING

Write the name of the offspring for each animal to complete the crossword puzzle. Use encyclopedias and other reference materials if you need help.

Across
2. deer
4. eagle
5. dog
7. giraffe
9. lion
11. swan
12. hog
13. cat
14. bobcat

Down
1. otter
3. zebra
5. turkey
6. fish
8. goose
10. ostrich

Just for Fun
Write the name of the offspring for each of these animals. Use an encyclopedia and other reference materials if you need help.

a. hawk _____

b. kangaroo _____

c. whale _____

d. rhinoceros _____

e. donkey _____

Name _____ Date _____

Science Puzzle

SCIENCE, VOCABULARY, AND SPELLING

Write the science word that matches each definition to complete the crossword puzzle. Use the words in the box if you need help.

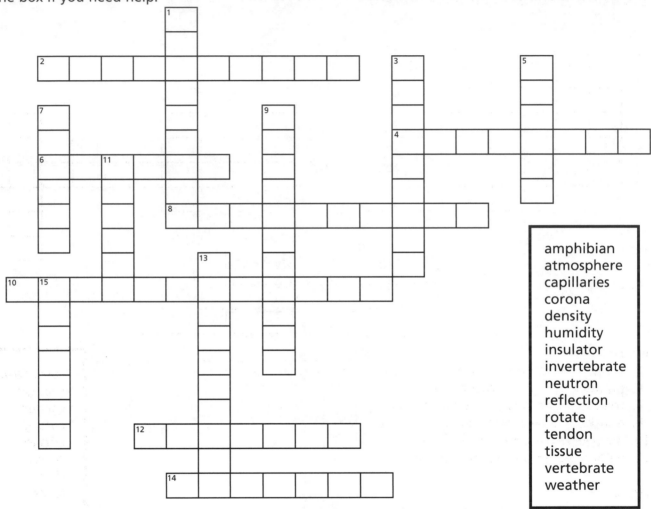

amphibian
atmosphere
capillaries
corona
density
humidity
insulator
invertebrate
neutron
reflection
rotate
tendon
tissue
vertebrate
weather

Across
2. all the air around the earth
4. the amount of moisture, or water, in the air
6. what the Earth does on its axis; spin
8. light energy that bounces off objects
10. an animal without a backbone
12. the condition of the atmosphere at any moment
14. the concentration of matter in an object

Down
1. material that does not conduct electricity
3. an animal with moist skin and no scales
5. a tough band of connective tissue that attaches a muscle to a bone
7. the sun's atmosphere
9. tiny blood vessels that join arteries and the veins
11. cells that work together to perform a specific function
13. an animal with a backbone
15. a subatomic particle with no charge

Just for Fun
Make a word search puzzle (with an answer key) for a friend, using the fifteen science words from the word box. Hide your words going up, down, backward, forward, and diagonally.

Word Games • 6–8 • © 2005 Creative Teaching Press

Name _____ Date _____

Insect Puzzle

SCIENCE, VOCABULARY, AND SPELLING

Write the name of the insect that matches each description to complete the crossword puzzle. Use the words in the box if you need help.

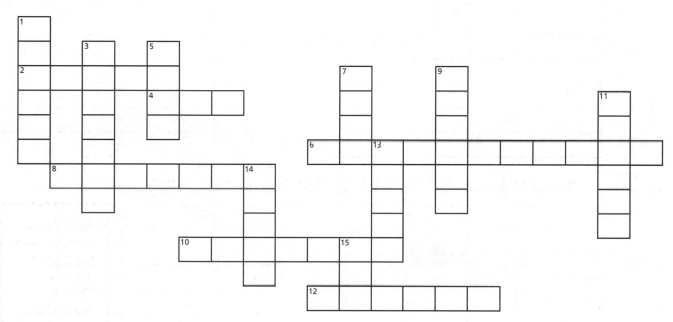

Across

2. a wormlike animal that hatches from an insect's egg
4. number of legs an insect has
6. the larva of a butterfly or moth
8. another name for an insect's antennae
10. an insect that eats wood
12. a silky case spun by a caterpillar

Down

1. a group of ants living together
3. an insect that makes a chirping sound
5. an insect that stings
7. a small, biting insect that can't fly but can jump far
9. the middle part of an insect's body
11. what the word metamorphosis means
13. the number of main body parts an insect has
14. a large number of bees, led by a queen, leaving a hive to start a new colony
15. the number of pairs of wings a butterfly has

| caterpillar |
| change |
| cocoon |
| colony |
| cricket |
| feelers |
| flea |
| larva |
| six |
| swarm |
| termite |
| thorax |
| three |
| two |
| wasp |

Just for Fun

Do research and learn more about one of these insects: a katydid, a grasshopper, a beetle, a dragonfly, a fire ant, or a wasp. Write 20 fascinating facts about the insect you selected, and share your findings with your classmates in an oral report along with visual aids.

Name _____ Date _____

Number, Please

Vocabulary, Spelling, Weight, Measurement, and Time

Write the name of the weight, measurement, or time word that matches each description to complete the crossword puzzle. Some numbers may be used more than once. Use reference materials if you need help.

Across
2. number of ounces in a pound
4. number of years in a decade
6. number of minutes in an hour
8. number of feet in a yard
10. number of days in a week
12. number of square feet in a square yard
14. number of pints in a quart

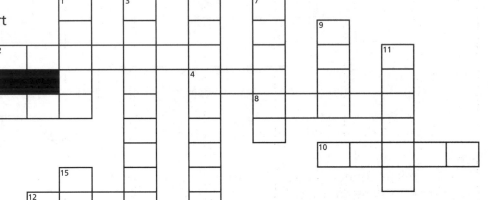

Down
1. number of seconds in a minute
3. number of years in a century
5. number of hours in a day
7. number of years in a score
9. number of quarts in a gallon
11. number of inches in a foot
13. 72 months equal how many years?
15. number of cups in two quarts

Just for Fun
Write the missing numbers.

a. _____ teaspoons = 3 tablespoons

b. _____ cups = 2 pints

c. _____ hours = 2 days

d. _____ years = 3 centuries

e. _____ pounds = 2 tons

Word Games • 6–8 © 2005 Creative Teaching Press

Name _____ Date _____

What Would You Do with an Apiary?

VOCABULARY

What would you do with each of the following things whose names are printed in bold? Find and circle the best answer in each group of words. Use a dictionary if you need help.

1 What would you do with an **apiary**?
   a. go there to get a haircut
   b. go to the dentist with it
   c. keep apes in cages there
   d. keep bees and their hives there

2 What would you do with an **alder**?
   a. plant it
   b. light candles on it
   c. get a cage for it
   d. wear it to the beach

3 What would you do with an **abacus**?
   a. dial it
   b. drain spaghetti in it
   c. strum music on it
   d. do arithmetic on it

4 What would you do with an **admiral**?
   a. admire it in a store window
   b. wear it on your head or around your neck
   c. salute him or her
   d. treat it with antibiotics

5 What would you do with an **agate**?
   a. lock it
   b. use it in making jewelry
   c. attach it to a wooden gate
   d. rake leaves with it

6 What would you do with an **atoll**?
   a. measure liquids in it
   b. chop it up for a salad
   c. reach it by boat
   d. pay a fee to use a freeway or highway

7 What would you do with an **auxiliary**?
   a. powder a baby with it
   b. serve it as a snack
   c. lend support to a group or an organization
   d. polish it to keep it shiny

8 What would you do with **arbitration**?
   a. follow its ruling to settle a dispute
   b. celebrate a holiday with it
   c. use it to pour concrete
   d. give a false impression

9 What would you do with an **accountant**?
   a. do algebra on it
   b. have him or her prepare your taxes
   c. go to him or her for medical treatment
   d. take a ride in it

10 What would you do with **apparel**?
   a. bang the two of them together
   b. add it to a car's engine
   c. buckle it up
   d. wear it

Name _____ Date _____

What Would You Do with a Buoy?

Vocabulary

What would you do with each of the following things whose names are printed in bold? Find and circle the best answer in each group of words. Use a dictionary if you need help.

1 What would you do with a **buoy**?
   a. use it to lift heavy objects
   b. hang it on the ceiling for light
   c. float it in water to warn of danger
   d. bathe it

2 What would you do with **burlap**?
   a. glue things with it
   b. make furniture with it
   c. use it to make sacks or bags
   d. serve it at dinnertime

3 What would you do at a **bazaar**?
   a. ski down it in the winter
   b. buy or sell many different kinds of things
   c. be careful not to prick yourself on its thorns
   d. attach it to your pet's collar

4 What would you do with **badminton**?
   a. play it using a racket
   b. play it in the school band
   c. barbecue it
   d. sweep it up and throw it away

5 What would you do with **ballast**?
   a. write a school essay with it
   b. use it to steady or balance a ship
   c. use it to repair a television set
   d. use it while performing a ballet

6 What would you do with a **bangle**?
   a. bang it against a metal drum
   b. eat it with lox and cream cheese
   c. wear it on your wrist or ankle
   d. blow into it

7 What would you do with **bifocals**?
   a. wear them to see better
   b. wear them to straighten your teeth
   c. wear them on your feet
   d. wear them to warm your hands

8 What would you do with a **bridle**?
   a. watch her walk down the aisle
   b. bake it in the oven
   c. chew it
   d. put it on a horse's head

9 What would you do with a **bribe**?
   a. put it on a baby to keep him or her clean while eating
   b. put it on your calendar
   c. offer it to someone for something you want him or her to do
   d. deposit it in a bank

10 What would you do with a **boulevard**?
   a. drive a car on it
   b. fight a duel with it
   c. grow tomatoes on it
   d. keep a farm animal inside it

Word Games • 6–8 © 2005 Creative Teaching Press

Name _____ Date _____

What Would You Do with a Dais?

VOCABULARY

What would you do with each of the following things whose names are printed in bold? Find and circle the best answer in each group of words. Use a dictionary if you need help.

1 What would you do with a **dais**?
   a. take a ride through a park in it
   b. blend or chop food with it
   c. water it on a daily basis
   d. stand on it to be seen better

2 What would you do with a **depot**?
   a. go there to get a bus or train
   b. try to remove him or her from office
   c. use it to construct a house
   d. heat liquids in it

3 What would you do with a **dinghy**?
   a. ring it to call people to dinner
   b. measure with it
   c. take a ride on a lake in it
   d. see it in a tropical rain forest

4 What would you do with a **discus**?
   a. serve food on it
   b. throw it
   c. look at it under a microscope
   d. use it to converse with another person

5 What would you do with a **dredge**?
   a. use it to move a heavy object
   b. pound meat with it to flatten it
   c. sift flour with it when baking
   d. scoop up mud from the bottom of a lake

6 What would you do with a **decoy**?
   a. use it to catch fish
   b. use it to hoist a flag on a pole
   c. lure someone or something with it
   d. play it in your back yard

7 What would you do with a **diphthong**?
   a. wash it in soapy water
   b. wear it to the beach
   c. dip fruit in it with a skewer
   d. pronounce it

8 What would you do with **defiance**?
   a. finance it with a bank
   b. oppose a powerful person or thing
   c. explain something not understood
   d. respect a person or thing

9 What would you do if you made a **descent**?
   a. moved upward
   b. removed a foul odor in a room
   c. earned a decent salary
   d. moved downward

10 What would you do if you **dissented**?
   a. disagreed
   b. fell apart
   c. ignored someone or something
   d. disposed of something

What Would You Do with a Fathom?

VOCABULARY

What would you do with each of the following things whose names are printed in bold? Find and circle the best answer in each group of words. Use a dictionary if you need help.

1 What would you do with a **fathom**?
   a. use it to measure air pressure
   b. attach it to a buggy
   c. use it as a measure for the depth of water
   d. kick it into the air

2 What would you do with a **ferret**?
   a. wear it on your head in winter
   b. look at it under a magnifying glass
   c. drink juice in it
   d. keep it as a pet

3 What would you do with a **fiend**?
   a. stay as far away as possible from him or her
   b. buy it in a department store
   c. put it in the refrigerator to keep it cold
   d. use it to change a light bulb

4 What would you do in a **foundry**?
   a. clean dirty laundry
   b. find lost items
   c. look at stars and planets
   d. melt metal and cast it into different shapes

5 What would you do with a **forsythia**?
   a. put it in a cage and feed it
   b. lace hiking boots with it
   c. plant it
   d. sprinkle it on a steak for flavor

6 What would you do with a **foal**?
   a. get a penalty for it in football
   b. take a picture of it with its mother
   c. knit a blanket or sweater with it
   d. watch it fly away

7 What would you do with a **fritter**?
   a. eat it
   b. swat it
   c. strain food with it to get rid of lumps
   d. attach it to a bicycle chain

8 What would you do during a **famine**?
   a. become famous
   b. fan yourself on a hot day
   c. go hungry
   d. paste it in a family photo album

9 What would you do with a **finch**?
   a. tighten a loose pipe with it
   b. scatter seeds for it to eat
   c. use it to mix cake batter
   d. staple it

10 What would you do with a **figurine**?
   a. use it to take your measurements
   b. find it on the bow of a ship
   c. wear it on a sweater
   d. put it on a shelf in your living room

What Would You Do with a Kiwi?

VOCABULARY

What would you do with each of the following things whose names are printed in bold? Find and circle the best answer in each group of words. Use a dictionary if you need help.

1 What would you do with a **kiwi**?
   a. visit it in a New Zealand zoo
   b. use it to tell time
   c. play a tune on it by strumming it
   d. drink it if you were in China

2 What would you do with a **kiln**?
   a. take a bath in it
   b. put seeds in it to feed the birds
   c. toast bread in it
   d. bake bricks or pottery in it

3 What would you do with a **kumquat**?
   a. sing it
   b. watch it swim in the ocean
   c. dance to it
   d. eat it

4 What would you do with a **knickknack**?
   a. carry things in it when hiking
   b. play it in a calypso band
   c. display it
   d. use it as a door knocker

5 What would you do with a **ketch**?
   a. put medicine on it
   b. put it on a hamburger for flavor
   c. sail in it
   d. boil water in it

6 What would you do with **kindling**?
   a. use it to start a fire
   b. play it as a board game
   c. eat it for a snack
   d. fly it

7 What would you do with a **kilowatt**?
   a. spray it
   b. measure tire pressure with it
   c. use it as a measure of electrical power
   d. put ammunition in it

8 What would you do with **kin**?
   a. dice it up and toss it in a salad
   b. light it for atmosphere
   c. feed it to goldfish
   d. invite them to a family reunion

9 What would you do with a **katydid**?
   a. make an appointment with it
   b. compare it to a grasshopper
   c. scrub it
   d. exercise on it at the gym

10 What would you do with a **kerchief**?
   a. sharpen it so it doesn't become dull
   b. start a dead car battery with it
   c. look at it through a telescope
   d. wear it around your neck or head

Name _____ Date _____

What Would You Do with a Larder?

VOCABULARY

What would you do with each of the following things whose names are printed in bold? Find and circle the best answer in each group of words. Use a dictionary if you need help.

1 What would you do with a **larder**?
a. use it to capture a stray dog
b. store food in it
c. spread it on toast
d. use it to climb on a roof

2 What would you do with a **landmark**?
a. visit it while on a vacation
b. use it to survey property
c. write on it with chalk
d. land a helicopter on it

3 What would you do with **laryngitis**?
a. soak it in hot water
b. play it in an orchestra
c. wrap your swollen foot in it
d. whisper instead of talk

4 What would you do with a **leaflet**?
a. paint with it
b. freeze it
c. read it
d. use it as bait for fishing

5 What would you do with a **lariat**?
a. watch it hop on two, strong hind legs
b. twirl it
c. put it on your finger
d. light it when camping

6 What would you do with **lacrosse**?
a. play it on a field
b. fight with it while on horseback
c. dance it
d. chew it

7 What would you do with **lacquer**?
a. mix it with icing while frosting a cake
b. play it in the school band
c. put it on metal or wood for a glossy finish
d. use it to remove grease or oil stains

8 What would you do with a **lynx**?
a. buy it in a jewelry store
b. put it in a vase
c. repair a computer with it
d. see it in a zoo

9 What would you do with a **loon**?
a. make balloons out of it
b. watch it dive with its pointed bill
c. weave on it
d. watch it slither in the grass

10 What would you do with **licorice**?
a. eat it
b. powder your face with it
c. apply for it when driving a car
d. drink it with sugar and cream

Word Games • 6–8 © 2005 Creative Teaching Press

What Would You Do with a Nozzle?

Vocabulary

What would you do with each of the following things whose names are printed in bold? Find and circle the best answer in each group of words. Use a dictionary if you need help.

1 What would you do with a **nozzle**?
- **a.** feed it tiny insects
- **b.** put it on the end of a hose or pipe
- **c.** use it to blow your nose
- **d.** use it while cooking

2 What would you do with a **narrative**?
- **a.** repair it using a screwdriver
- **b.** write it
- **c.** sing it in an opera
- **d.** paint it

3 What would you do with a **nasturtium**?
- **a.** plant it
- **b.** play music on it
- **c.** wear it
- **d.** weigh it

4 What would you do with a **nettle**?
- **a.** use it to catch lobsters and crabs
- **b.** use it to keep your hair neat
- **c.** cook food in it
- **d.** be careful not to touch its leaves

5 What would you do if you were **nocturnal**?
- **a.** be sailing on the ocean
- **b.** be active during the daytime
- **c.** be active at night
- **d.** hibernate in the winter

6 What would you do with a **notion**?
- **a.** use it to soften your hands
- **b.** have a sharp pain
- **c.** use it to polish furniture
- **d.** have a general idea

7 What would you do if you were **nimble**?
- **a.** move slowly and ploddingly
- **b.** move quickly and lightly
- **c.** be able to sew very well
- **d.** be forgetful

8 What would you do with a **nibble**?
- **a.** feed it to your pet rabbit
- **b.** jump rope with it
- **c.** put it on a baby's bottle
- **d.** just eat a small bite

9 What would you do with a **nectarine**?
- **a.** tie it around your neck
- **b.** blow into it to make music
- **c.** peel it and eat it
- **d.** shake it and hear its bells ring

10 What would you do if you were **neutral**?
- **a.** be very pale and lifeless
- **b.** be unable to be in tight, closed-inplaces
- **c.** not be organized
- **d.** not take either side in a dispute

What Would You Do with a Scull?

VOCABULARY

What would you do with each of the following things whose names are printed in bold? Find and circle the best answer in each group of words. Use a dictionary if you need help.

1 What would you do with a **scull**?
   a. fry it in oil
   b. play it on the school blacktop
   c. pull it out of the ground
   d. use it for rowing

2 What would you do with a **saga**?
   a. put it out in the sun to dry out
   b. listen to it or read it
   c. wear it around your waist
   d. spray it with fertilizer

3 What would you do with **salve**?
   a. paint with it
   b. skate on it
   c. put it on a hot dog or hamburger
   d. put it on a wound

4 What would you do with a **scallion**?
   a. cut it up for a salad
   b. photograph it in a zoo
   c. see it at the beach
   d. stand on it when painting a wall

5 What would you do with a **shanty**?
   a. place it on your head
   b. wear it on your foot
   c. float on the water with it
   d. go inside it to get out of the sun

6 What would you do with a **sage**?
   a. respect and admire him or her
   b. put it in a birdcage
   c. sit on it
   d. climb it to reach a top shelf

7 What would you do with a **sapphire**?
   a. drink it with lemon
   b. season a steak with it
   c. wear it to a fancy party
   d. play it using a deck of cards

8 What would you do with a **silo**?
   a. store food for cattle in it
   b. wipe a kitchen counter with it
   c. sing it by yourself
   d. use it to take a nail out of the wall

9 What would you do with **slush**?
   a. use it for painting a picture
   b. bake it in an oven
   c. go to the doctor for treatment
   d. be careful not to slip on it in the winter

10 What would you do with a **spigot**?
   a. feed it corn from a trough
   b. pet it
   c. turn it on to get water
   d. go fishing for it

Word Games • 6–8 © 2005 Creative Teaching Press

Name _____   Date _____

What Would You Do with a Torrent?

VOCABULARY

What would you do with each of the following things whose names are printed in bold? Find and circle the best answer in each group of words. Use a dictionary if you need help.

1 What would you do with a **torrent**?
  a. use it to open a package
  b. put a paper clip on it
  c. protect yourself with an umbrella
  d. attach it to the roof of a car

2 What would you do with a **transmitter**?
  a. send out sounds or signals
  b. use it to mow a lawn
  c. take a ride on it
  d. sail on the ocean on it

3 What would you do with a **transom**?
  a. use it when putting up wallpaper
  b. paint with it
  c. fly it
  d. open it to get more air

4 What would you do with a **trapezoid**?
  a. use it to knit a scarf
  b. measure it in math class
  c. view it under a microscope
  d. cage it

5 What would you do with **tuition**?
  a. have a hunch or idea about something
  b. try out for a part in a play
  c. take a standardized test
  d. pay it to a college or private school

6 What would you do with a **token**?
  a. use it to pay for a ride on a bus or subway
  b. slice it very thin and put it on bread
  c. write a letter with it
  d. wear it in your hair

7 What would you do with a **tether**?
  a. put it on your teeth to straighten them
  b. use it to keep your dog in your yard
  c. use it in a game of badminton
  d. anchor a ship with it

8 What would you do with a **tier**?
  a. wrap a present with it
  b. use it to wipe your eyes
  c. wear it on your head like a crown
  d. layer it atop another one

9 What would you do with **tradition**?
  a. swallow it when you are sick
  b. store things in it
  c. hand it down from generation to generation
  d. put it on an envelope

10 What would you do with a **tract**?
  a. plant crops in it
  b. take a ride in it
  c. boil it
  d. nail it into a wall

What Would You Do with a Vandal?

Vocabulary

What would you do with each of the following things whose names are printed in bold? Find and circle the best answer in each group of words. Use a dictionary if you need help.

1) What would you do with a **vandal**?
a. wear it on your foot at the beach
b. arrest him or her
c. pack things in it to take on a trip
d. play it with friends

2) What would you do with a **vacancy**?
a. put it in a playpen
b. find it on a menu at a restaurant
c. try to fill it
d. rinse it out

3) What would you do with **vault**?
a. keep money or valuables in it
b. barbecue on it
c. sharpen a pencil with it
d. tell the direction of the wind with it

4) What would you do with **velvet**?
a. put it between two pieces of bread
b. hammer it
c. pour it over your head
d. use it to make a fancy dress

5) What would you do with a **veranda**?
a. dance it to fast, upbeat music
b. play it in an orchestra
c. sit on it on a summer night
d. take it to a mechanic

6) What would you do with a **visa**?
a. wear it to block the sun from your face
b. blow it to call your dog inside
c. enjoy the view from it
d. show it to enter a foreign country

7) What would you do with a **vulture**?
a. photograph it at the zoo
b. turn it on to light up a room
c. pack it for your vacation
d. hit it over a net to an opposing team

8) What would you do with a **vocalist**?
a. listen to him or her sing a song
b. play it
c. spray your throat with it
d. recite it in class

9) What would you do with **vinegar**?
a. grow it on a vine
b. sharpen a knife with it
c. put it in your car's engine
d. flavor foods with it

10) What would you do with a **vessel**?
a. put it on under a shirt
b. hold something in it
c. eat dinner under it
d. put it on a calendar

Word Games • 6–8 © 2005 Creative Teaching Press

Ladder Links #1

VOCABULARY AND SPELLING

The object of a ladder link puzzle is to change one word into another by changing only one letter at a time. You cannot change the order of the letters. Here is an example of a ladder link:

F E A R
<u>D</u> E A R   (the F has been changed to D; the other letters remain the same)
D E <u>E</u> R   (the A has been changed to E)
D E E <u>P</u>   (the R has been changed to P)

1 Change HOME into CART.

H	O	M	E
C	A	R	T

(homophone for the word **sum**)

(alike; identical)

(past tense of come)

(a group of tents or huts to live in for a time)

(to complain or find fault in a nagging way)

2 Change LOON into HEAR.

L	O	O	N
H	E	A	R

(something, such as money, that is lent)

(held at one time)

(a homophone for rode)

(to speak written words aloud)

(the part of the body that contains the brain, eyes, ears, nose, and mouth)

Ladder Links #2

Vocabulary and Spelling

The object of a ladder link puzzle is to change one word into another by changing only one letter at a time. You cannot change the order of the letters.

1) Change SACK into PINT.

S	A	C	K
P	I	N	T

(shortage; a need for something that is missing)

(a delicate fabric of fine thread woven into fancy designs)

(a step in walking or running)

(a homophone for pain)

(an evergreen tree)

2) Change PAPER into WORDS.

P	A	P	E	R
W	O	R	D	S

(a playful or silly trick; prank)

(pieces of land that stick out into a sea or lake)

(deals with successfully)

(the central or most important parts of things)

(thick strings or ropes)

Word Games • 6–8 © 2005 Creative Teaching Press

Ladder Links #3

VOCABULARY AND SPELLING

The object of a ladder link puzzle is to change one word into another by changing only one letter at a time. You cannot change the order of the letters.

1 Change HURL into TAME.

H	U	R	L
T	A	M	E

(to cause pain or harm to; to wound)

(rudely short or abrupt in manner or speech)

(a treatment or remedy)

(worry or concern)

(past tense of come)

(the condition of being well known)

2 Change TINT into DIME.

T	I	N	T
D	I	M	E

(fuzzy, short fabric fibers)

(group of words spoken by an actor)

(the plural of louse)

(the seeds or grain of a kind of grass)

(small cubes marked with dots on each side)

Ladder Links #4

VOCABULARY AND SPELLING

The object of a ladder link puzzle is to change one word into another by changing only one letter at a time. You cannot change the order of the letters.

1 Change BEND into GAME.

B	E	N	D
G	A	M	E

(to cause to be carried or delivered)

(tiny, loose grains worn away from rocks)

(having a sound, healthy mind)

(alike in some way)

(past tense of come)

2 Change Change PICK into GATE.

P	I	C	K
G	A	T	E

(a bundle of things tied together for carrying)

(framework for hanging or displaying things)

(a contest to see who can go the fastest)

(a tool that has a long handle and prongs at one end)

(the speed or velocity of something)

Word Games • 6–8 © 2005 Creative Teaching Press

Ladder Links #5

Vocabulary and Spelling

The object of a ladder link puzzle is to change one word into another by changing only one letter at a time. You cannot change the order of the letters.

1 Change BOOK into MEAT.

B	O	O	K
M	E	A	T

(a covering for the foot and part of the leg)

(a ship of any size)

(the fur or skin of an animal)

(an animal related to a sheep that chews its cud)

(a deep, wide ditch dug around a castle)

2 Change HOST into BIKE.

H	O	S	T
B	I	K	E

(price)

(to throw out or down; toss)

(a container for holding something)

(a baked food made from a sweetened batter)

(to get hold of; grasp)

(to cook food in an oven)

Word Games • 6–8 © 2005 Creative Teaching Press

Ladder Links #6

SPELLING

The object of a ladder link puzzle is to change one word into another by changing only one letter at a time. You cannot change the order of the letters. To help you solve the puzzle, the letter that should be changed on each line has been shaded.

1 Change NEVER into TIMES.

N	E	V	E	R
T	I	M	E	S

3 Change BLEND into TREAT.

B	L	E	N	D
T	R	E	A	T

2 Change HARD into EASE.

H	A	R	D
E	A	S	E

4 Change STORY into SHARP.

S	T	O	R	Y
S	H	A	R	P

Word Games • 6–8 © 2005 Creative Teaching Press

Ladder Links #7

SPELLING

The object of a ladder link puzzle is to change one word into another by changing only one letter at a time. You cannot change the order of the letters. To help you solve the puzzle, the letter that should be changed on each line has been shaded.

1 Change CHEW into SLED.

C	H	E	W
S	L	E	D

3 Change NOVEL into COMET.

N	O	V	E	L
C	O	M	E	T

2 Change BLANK into GRAIN.

B	L	A	N	K
G	R	A	I	N

4 Change BOOM into SOIL.

B	O	O	M
S	O	I	L

Name _____   Date _____

Ladder Links #8

VOCABULARY AND SPELLING

The object of a ladder link puzzle is to change one word into another by changing only one letter at a time. You cannot change the order of the letters. To help you solve the puzzle, the letter that should be changed on each line has been shaded.

1 Change BEAT into MANE.

B	E	A	T
M	A	N	E

2 Change WARM into COLD.

W	A	R	M
C	O	L	D

3 Change TRUCE into BRISK.

T	R	U	C	E
B	R	I	S	K

4 Change GOAD into CLIP.

G	O	A	D
C	L	I	P

Name _____ Date _____

Ladder Links #9

Vocabulary and Spelling

The object of a ladder link puzzle is to change one word into another by changing only one letter at a time. You cannot change the order of the letters. To help you solve the puzzle, the letter that should be changed on each line has been shaded.

1 Change TOOL into BALE.

T	O	O	L
B	A	L	E

3 Change SCENE into PLANT.

S	C	E	N	E
P	L	A	N	T

2 Change SAGE into WELL.

S	A	G	E
W	E	L	L

4 Change DART into SOLE.

D	A	R	T
S	O	L	E

Ladder Links #10

SPELLING

The object of a ladder link puzzle is to change one word into another by changing only one letter at a time. You cannot change the order of the letters. To help you solve the puzzle, the letter that should be changed on each line has been shaded.

1 Change COAL into FINE.

C	O	A	L
F	I	N	E

3 Change WRITE into DRINK.

W	R	I	T	E
D	R	I	N	K

2 Change WHALE into SPOUT.

W	H	A	L	E
S	P	O	U	T

4 Change HOOK into SIFT.

H	O	O	K
S	I	F	T

Word Games • 6–8 © 2005 Creative Teaching Press

Noun Analogies

VOCABULARY AND NOUNS

An **analogy** is the relationship between one pair of words that serves as the basis for the creation of another pair of words. Find the word that best completes each analogy. Circle the letter of your word choice. Use a dictionary if you need help.

1 iguana : reptile :: katydid :
   a. fish
   b. lizard
   c. grasshopper
   d. insect

2 atlas : maps :: dictionary :
   a. words
   b. encyclopedias
   c. books
   d. libraries

3 route : course :: blemish :
   a. blush
   b. face
   c. flaw
   d. powder

4 viola : instrument :: cirrus :
   a. circus
   b. cloud
   c. star
   d. tree

5 cardigan : sweater :: loafer :
   a. shoe
   b. hat
   c. shawl
   d. skirt

6 ounce : pound :: year :
   a. minute
   b. yard
   c. second
   d. decade

7 reign : rain :: quarts :
   a. gallon
   b. quartz
   c. pint
   d. fractions

8 zinnia : flower :: puffin :
   a. amphibian
   b. tiger
   c. fish
   d. bird

9 devotion : loyalty :: ordinance :
   a. judge
   b. law
   c. order
   d. court

10 elbow : arm :: femur :
   a. hand
   b. shoulder
   c. leg
   d. skull

Name _____ Date _____

Verb Analogies

Vocabulary and Verbs

An **analogy** is the relationship between one pair of words that serves as the basis for the creation of another pair of words. Find the word that best completes each analogy. Circle the letter of your word choice. Use a dictionary if you need help.

1 endorse : approve :: divulge :
- **a.** soothe
- **b.** extend
- **c.** tell
- **d.** dive

2 resist : comply :: retreat :
- **a.** eat
- **b.** advance
- **c.** withdraw
- **d.** defend

3 vanish : disappear :: alter :
- **a.** modify
- **b.** altar
- **c.** inquire
- **d.** elect

4 forgive : pardon :: stifle :
- **a.** stiffen
- **b.** sniffle
- **c.** suppress
- **d.** pass

5 pulsate : throb :: babble :
- **a.** bubble
- **b.** giggle
- **c.** boil
- **d.** chatter

6 omit : include :: swell :
- **a.** shrink
- **b.** expand
- **c.** swallow
- **d.** mend

7 imitate : copy :: sulk :
- **a.** twist
- **b.** pout
- **c.** pour
- **d.** return

8 condone : ignore :: squander :
- **a.** waste
- **b.** squat
- **c.** proclaim
- **d.** invest

9 mumble : enunciate :: ignite :
- **a.** fire
- **b.** invigorate
- **c.** eject
- **d.** extinguish

10 reiterate : repeat :: mock :
- **a.** ridicule
- **b.** ruin
- **c.** meet
- **d.** divert

Word Games • 6–8 © 2005 Creative Teaching Press

Adjective Analogies

VOCABULARY AND ADJECTIVES

An **analogy** is the relationship between one pair of words that serves as the basis for the creation of another pair of words. Find the word that best completes each analogy. Circle the letter of your word choice. Use a dictionary if you need help.

1 easy : difficult :: ambitious :
a. clever
b. enormous
c. lazy
d. steady

2 tranquil : peaceful :: sensible :
a. foolish
b. sensitive
c. thrifty
d. wise

3 messy : tidy :: sullen :
a. mean
b. jovial
c. depressing
d. moody

4 nimble : agile :: limp :
a. slack
b. plump
c. tight
d. light

5 benevolent : charitable :: obvious :
a. obsolete
b. foolish
c. oblivious
d. apparent

6 gaunt : thin :: exact :
a. quiet
b. precise
c. confident
d. agreeable

7 punctual : prompt :: placid:
a. excited
b. calm
c. plain
d. showy

8 ominous : threatening :: explicit :
a. hasty
b. prosperous
c. faithful
d. definite

9 frivolous : serious :: obscure :
a. hidden
b. distinct
c. obtuse
d. blurry

10 eerie : spooky :: vivacious :
a. lively
b. vivid
c. uncertain
d. nebulous

Word Games • 6–8 © 2005 Creative Teaching Press

Analogy Challenge #1

Vocabulary

An **analogy** is the relationship between one pair of words that serves as the basis for the creation of another pair of words. Find the word that best completes each analogy. Circle the letter of your word choice. Use a dictionary if you need help.

1 lamb : sheep :: fawn :
   a. chick
   b. deer
   c. horse
   d. pet

2 meteorologist : weather :: geologist :
   a. astronomy
   b. vertebrates
   c. flowers
   d. rocks

3 vermilion : red :: ebony :
   a. black
   b. brown
   c. ivory
   d. blue

4 quartet : four :: duet :
   a. waltz
   b. two
   c. song
   d. six

5 carrot : carat :: oar :
   a. canoe
   b. paddle
   c. ore
   d. gold

6 prior : previous :: negotiate :
   a. bargain
   b. adjourn
   c. neutralize
   d. intimidate

7 spoke : wheel :: radius :
   a. compass
   b. circle
   c. circumference
   d. radical

8 aquarium : fish :: terrarium :
   a. tiger
   b. reptile
   c. bird
   d. plant

9 hermit : recluse :: miner :
   a. gold
   b. minor
   c. prospector
   d. tunnel

10 flag : pole :: sail :
   a. pail
   b. sale
   c. mast
   d. ocean

Word Games • 6–8 © 2005 Creative Teaching Press

Analogy Challenge #2

VOCABULARY

An **analogy** is the relationship between one pair of words that serves as the basis for the creation of another pair of words. Find the word that best completes each analogy. Circle the letter of your word choice. Use a dictionary if you need help.

1 indigo : blue :: crimson :
- **a.** green
- **b.** black
- **c.** red
- **d.** brown

2 feet : yard :: month :
- **a.** minute
- **b.** pound
- **c.** year
- **d.** mouth

3 sun : star :: Earth :
- **a.** land
- **b.** round
- **c.** planet
- **d.** moon

4 thermometer : temperature :: barometer :
- **a.** air pressure
- **b.** distance
- **c.** rate of speed
- **d.** water levels

5 veil : vale :: marshal :
- **a.** sheriff
- **b.** martial
- **c.** marsh
- **d.** police

6 envious : jealous :: arrogant :
- **a.** angry
- **b.** bossy
- **c.** timid
- **d.** haughty

7 wing : airplane :: tire :
- **a.** exhausted
- **b.** truck
- **c.** spoke
- **d.** rubber

8 coyote : desert :: porpoise :
- **a.** ocean
- **b.** dolphin
- **c.** mammal
- **d.** purpose

9 brush : artist :: baton :
- **a.** bat
- **b.** surgeon
- **c.** plumber
- **d.** conductor

10 kale : vegetable :: mango :
- **a.** meat
- **b.** fruit
- **c.** dance
- **d.** orange

Analogy Challenge #3

VOCABULARY

An **analogy** is the relationship between one pair of words that serves as the basis for the creation of another pair of words. Find the word that best completes each analogy. Circle the letter of your word choice. Use a dictionary if you need help.

1 pail : water :: hamper :
   a. clothes
   b. prevent
   c. hinder
   d. tamper

2 ox : oxen :: moose :
   a. mooses
   b. antler
   c. moose
   d. moosess

3 sound : decibel :: electricity :
   a. static
   b. volt
   c. plug
   d. energy

4 drake : duck :: rooster :
   a. hen
   b. chicken
   c. bird
   d. crow

5 yam : tuber :: azalea :
   a. vegetable
   b. fruit
   c. fish
   d. flower

6 mouse : mice :: child :
   a. toddler
   b. childs
   c. children
   d. childes

7 idle : busy :: rude :
   a. abrupt
   b. polite
   c. nasty
   d. crude

8 straight : strait :: ewe :
   a. mammal
   b. animal
   c. goat
   d. yew

9 march : parade :: sing :
   a. opera
   b. dance
   c. tenor
   d. alto

10 keys : piano :: strings :
   a. drum
   b. trumpet
   c. cello
   d. cymbal

Word Games • 6–8 © 2005 Creative Teaching Press

Analogy Challenge #4

VOCABULARY

An **analogy** is the relationship between one pair of words that serves as the basis for the creation of another pair of words. Find the word that best completes each analogy. Circle the letter of your word choice. Use a dictionary if you need help.

1 burn : singe :: pardon :
   a. grant
   b. beg
   c. forgive
   d. parole

2 endive : lettuce :: leek :
   a. onion
   b. leak
   c. potato
   d. fruit

3 knead : dough :: poach :
   a. pouch
   b. roach
   c. purse
   d. egg

4 dwindle : expand :: humiliate :
   a. tease
   b. praise
   c. embarrass
   d. magnify

5 chews : choose :: palette :
   a. artist
   b. paint
   c. brush
   d. pallet

6 hive : bees :: colony :
   a. settlement
   b. spiders
   c. moths
   d. termites

7 ostrich : chick :: kangaroo :
   a. joey
   b. pouch
   c. cub
   d. kit

8 flock : chickens :: pack :
   a. luggage
   b. cats
   c. wolves
   d. bears

9 racket : tennis :: wicket :
   a. cricket
   b. football
   c. golf
   d. skiing

10 pupil : eye :: lobe :
   a. hand
   b. nose
   c. strobe
   d. ear

Word Games • 6–8 © 2005 Creative Teaching Press

Synonym and Antonym Analogies

Vocabulary, Synonyms, and Antonyms

An **analogy** is the relationship between one pair of words that serves as the basis for the creation of another pair of words. Find the word that best completes each analogy. Circle the letter of your word choice. Use a dictionary if you need help.

1 fraud : deception :: excursion :
- **a.** jaunt
- **b.** excuse
- **c.** temptation
- **d.** commotion

2 candid : frank :: staunch :
- **a.** heavy
- **b.** tender
- **c.** wealthy
- **d.** firm

3 laud : defame :: benign :
- **a.** beginning
- **b.** harmless
- **c.** honest
- **d.** malignant

4 pleasant : obnoxious :: attractive :
- **a.** beautiful
- **b.** repulsive
- **c.** magnetic
- **d.** attentive

5 ascent : descent :: abhor :
- **a.** detest
- **b.** hate
- **c.** destroy
- **d.** approve

6 permanent : temporary :: introvert :
- **a.** extrovert
- **b.** extraneous
- **c.** recluse
- **d.** invertebrate

7 thick : dense :: meager :
- **a.** many
- **b.** sparse
- **c.** merger
- **d.** ample

8 perspiration : sweat :: tempo :
- **a.** heat
- **b.** permanent
- **c.** drum
- **d.** beat

9 retreat : advance :: turbulent :
- **a.** rough
- **b.** calm
- **c.** bumpy
- **d.** merry

10 zeal : enthusiasm :: obstacle :
- **a.** obstruction
- **b.** assistance
- **c.** warning
- **d.** object

Word Games • 6–8 © 2005 Creative Teaching Press

Name _____ Date _____

On the Menu Analogies

VOCABULARY

An **analogy** is the relationship between one pair of words that serves as the basis for the creation of another pair of words. Find the word that best completes each analogy. Circle the letter of your word choice. Use a dictionary if you need help.

① turkey : poultry :: cow :
  a. milk
  b. bovine
  c. steer
  d. udder

② okra : vegetable :: kumquat :
  a. apple
  b. orange
  c. flsh
  d. fruit

③ mince : cut :: whip :
  a. beat
  b. fry
  c. dice
  d. bake

④ chocolate : sweet :: lemon :
  a. fruit
  b. yellow
  c. sour
  d. lime

⑤ ketchup : tomato :: cheese :
  a. cheddar
  b. milk
  c. yellow
  d. butter

⑥ tea : beverage :: tarragon :
  a. paprika
  b. salt
  c. liquid
  d. herb

⑦ ambrosia : coconut :: meringue :
  a. milk
  b. egg
  c. dessert
  d. lemon

⑧ spaghetti : meatball :: peanut butter :
  a. jelly
  b. nut
  c. sandwich
  d. fruit

⑨ pork : pig :: tuna :
  a. salmon
  b. fish
  c. steer
  d. squid

⑩ cereal : serial :: steak :
  a. barbecue
  b. stack
  c. beef
  d. stake

Name _____ Date _____

Sports Analogies

VOCABULARY

An **analogy** is the relationship between one pair of words that serves as the basis for the creation of another pair of words. Find the word that best completes each analogy. Circle the letter of your word choice. Use a dictionary if you need help.

1 row : canoe :: pedal :
   a. petal
   b. skateboard
   c. bicycle
   d. football

2 golf : gulf :: bowl :
   a. strike
   b. boll
   c. dish
   d. spare

3 grass : soccer :: ice :
   a. hockey
   b. frozen
   c. pool
   d. field

4 football : sport :: chess :
   a. knight
   b. board
   c. game
   d. rook

5 pro : amateur :: offense :
   a. advancement
   b. defense
   c. platoon
   d. squad

6 punt : football :: dribble :
   a. racket
   b. puck
   c. melt
   d. basketball

7 tennis : court :: wrestling :
   a. pin
   b. sport
   c. takedown
   d. mat

8 course : coarse :: chute :
   a. skiing
   b. tube
   c. slide
   d. shoot

9 strike : bowling :: goal :
   a. hockey
   b. archery
   c. badminton
   d. golf

10 referee : boxing :: umpire :
   a. coach
   b. referee
   c. baseball
   d. polo

Word Games • 6–8 © 2005 Creative Teaching Press

Name _____ Date _____

What's Hot?—What's Not? #1

CLASSIFYING AND VOCABULARY

The words in the "What's Hot?" column all have something in common. The words in the "What's Not?" column do not fit in the first group of words. Decide what the words in the first group have in common, and write the answer on the line.

What's Hot?   **What's Not?**

1 goldfish, fingernail, anyone   computer, grass, calendar
_____

2 sharply, quietly, legally   ugly, office, manipulate
_____

3 each, itself, mine   but, onto, except
_____

4 around, throughout, toward   everyone, neither, absent
_____

5 knew, began, wrote   begin, come, freeze
_____

6 tangy, bitter, salty   cloudy, faded, musty
_____

7 area, dedicated, razor   paper, open, white
_____

8 pound, brief, sun   secret, teacher, government
_____

9 give, be, shrink   done, bitten, torn
_____

10 refer, sees, level   repeat, scene, leave
_____

Just for Fun
Write five What's Hot?—What's Not? activities for a classmate to solve.

Word Games • 6–8 © 2005 Creative Teaching Press

Name _____ Date _____

What's Hot?—What's Not? #2

CLASSIFYING AND VOCABULARY

The words in the "What's Hot?" column all have something in common. The words in the "What's Not?" column do not fit in the first group of words. Decide what the words in the first group have in common, and write the answer on the line.

What's Hot?	**What's Not?**
1 jasmine, daffodil, geranium	gardener, tree, guppy
2 maroon, scarlet, crimson	cobalt, teal, hazel
3 archaic, antiquated, decrepit	archway, antifreeze, decree
4 canteen, kettle, urn	cantaloupe, knit, turn
5 limbo, tango, flamenco	gumbo, tangle, flame
6 peck, bushel, quart	cup, pint, ounce
7 slate, marble, gneiss	skate, glass, genius
8 straws, doughnuts, belts	notebook, cabinet, pencil
9 fly, diamond, inning	court, tackle, assist
10 zebu, gibbon, capybara	zipper, ribbon, copycat

Just for Fun
Write five What's Hot?—What's Not? activities for a classmate to solve.

Word Games • 6–8 © 2005 Creative Teaching Press

Continent, Please

Geography, Classifying, and Vocabulary

On which continent is each country located? Write the name of each country under the proper continent, and cross it off the list as you use each one. Use an atlas or map if you need help. *(Hint: There are six countries in each category.)*

Algeria	Chile	Liechtenstein
Andorra	Costa Rica	Mexico
Argentina	Cuba	Nepal
Austria	Czech Republic	Oman
Barbados	Djibouti	Pakistan
Belize	Ghana	Peru
Benin	Guyana	Poland
Bolivia	Greece	Turkey
Canada	Lebanon	Venezuela
Chad	Lesotho	Vietnam

North America	South America	Asia	Europe	Africa
_____	_____	_____	_____	_____
_____	_____	_____	_____	_____
_____	_____	_____	_____	_____
_____	_____	_____	_____	_____
_____	_____	_____	_____	_____
_____	_____	_____	_____	_____

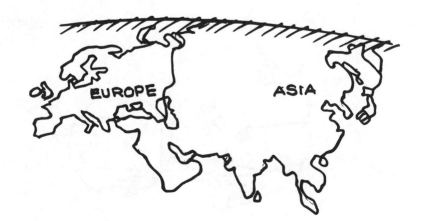

Geography Guru

Write the words under the proper categories, and cross them off the list as you use each one.
(Hint: There are six in each category.)

Florida	Montana
North America	Africa
China	Dallas
Los Angeles	Asia
Illinois	Japan
England	Rhode Island
South America	Santa Fe
Tennessee	Kenya
Boston	Baltimore
Brazil	Europe
Denver	Utah
Antarctica	Israel

city	state	country	continent
_____	_____	_____	_____
_____	_____	_____	_____
_____	_____	_____	_____
_____	_____	_____	_____
_____	_____	_____	_____
_____	_____	_____	_____

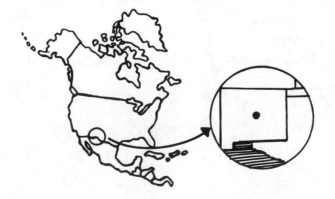

Word Games • 6–8 © 2005 Creative Teaching Press

Name _____ Date _____

Science Category Puzzle

CLASSIFYING AND VOCABULARY

Write the words under the proper categories, and cross them off the list as you use each one. Use a dictionary if you need help. *(Hint: There are six words in each category.)*

heron	guppy
tortoise	coyote
trout	yak
gnu	copperhead
flamingo	sloth
salmon	toucan
cobra	crocodile
condor	minnow
mackerel	hyena
koala	nightingale
lizard	barracuda
raven	alligator

mammal	**reptile**	**bird**	**fish**
_____	_____	_____	_____
_____	_____	_____	_____
_____	_____	_____	_____
_____	_____	_____	_____
_____	_____	_____	_____
_____	_____	_____	_____

Word Wizard

Parts of Speech, Classifying, and Vocabulary

Decide how each underlined word is used in the phrases.
Write the underlined words under the proper categories, and cross them off the list as you write
each one. *(Hint: There are six words in each category.)*

a <u>frightened</u> kitten
<u>two</u> teenagers
visits <u>regularly</u>
<u>is</u> invited
walked <u>away</u>
run an <u>errand</u>
<u>those</u> invoices
<u>three</u> pencils
went <u>upstairs</u>
<u>yawned</u> sleepily
<u>California</u> is
<u>had</u> eaten

<u>extinguished</u> the fire
<u>new</u> jacket
replied <u>sarcastically</u>
an <u>incredible</u> journey
his <u>happiness</u>
arriving <u>tomorrow</u>
<u>should</u> go
need a <u>signature</u>
this <u>house</u>
need <u>immediately</u>
<u>recommend</u> a restaurant
antique <u>table</u>

noun	verb	adjective	adverb
_____	_____	_____	_____
_____	_____	_____	_____
_____	_____	_____	_____
_____	_____	_____	_____
_____	_____	_____	_____
_____	_____	_____	_____

Word Games • 6–8 © 2005 Creative Teaching Press

Name _____ Date _____

Five-Letter Anagrams

SPELLING

An **anagram** is a rearrangement of the letters of one word to form another word.
Examples: serve—verse   lemon—melon

Write an anagram for each five-letter word.

1 large   _____

2 stove   _____

3 spins   _____

4 swipe   _____

5 charm   _____

6 filed   _____

7 zoned   _____

8 three   _____

9 sport   _____

10 ocean   _____

11 quiet   _____

12 roses   _____

 Just for Fun
How many other five-letter anagrams can you write? List them.

_____

_____

_____

Word Games • 6–8 © 2005 Creative Teaching Press

Name _____ Date _____

Six-Letter Anagrams

SPELLING

An **anagram** is a rearrangement of the letters of one word to form another word. Example: serves—verses

Write an anagram for each five-letter word.

1 lemons   _____

2 devote   _____

3 rustic   _____

4 rescue   _____

5 nights   _____

6 insect   _____

7 friend   _____

8 shaded   _____

9 adverb   _____

10 causes   _____

11 sister   _____

12 leader   _____

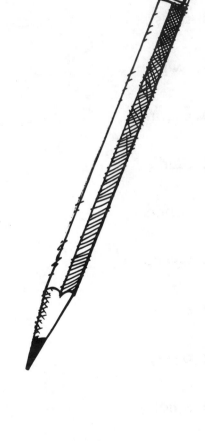

 Just for Fun
How many other six-letter anagrams can you write? List them.

_____

_____

_____

Word Games • 6–8 © 2005 Creative Teaching Press

Seven-Letter Anagrams

SPELLING

An **anagram** is a rearrangement of the letters of one word to form another word.
Example: density—destiny

Write an anagram for each seven-letter word.

1) reserve _____

2) antlers _____

3) infests _____

4) slipper _____

5) layered _____

6) sellers _____

7) silence _____

8) notices _____

9) senator _____

10) kitchen _____

11) heaters _____

12) remarks _____

 Just for Fun
How many other seven-letter anagrams can you write? List them.

_____

_____

_____

Eight-Letter Anagrams

SPELLING

An **anagram** is a rearrangement of the letters of one word to form another word.
Example: research—searcher

Write an anagram for each eight-letter word.

1 marching _____

2 hustling _____

3 cheating _____

4 misprint _____

5 oriental _____

6 salesman _____

7 needless _____

8 enlisted _____

9 organist _____

10 wreathes _____

11 articles _____

12 refining _____

 Just for Fun
How many other eight-letter anagrams can you write? List them.

_____

_____

_____

Word Games • 6–8 © 2005 Creative Teaching Press

Odd Word Out

VOCABULARY

In each row, find and circle the word that does not belong. Explain why it does not belong with the other words. Use a dictionary if you need help.

1	peony	palmetto	fuchsia	camellia	wisteria
2	off	around	above	upon	none
3	alabaster	celadon	mauve	skate	lavender
4	pretext	glossary	bibliography	preface	index
5	icing	hat trick	huddle	offside	face-off
6	sauté	cuddle	simmer	boil	baste
7	basalt	coal	granite	obsidian	pumice
8	derrick	pulley	wedge	turbine	pullet
9	asteroid	nebula	plane	comet	planet
10	condominium	palace	duplex	tepee	patio
11	Amazon	Nile	Kenya	Yangtze	Danube
12	neither	some	since	each	your
13	Jasper	Alberta	Ontario	Quebec	Manitoba
14	New Zealand	Europe	Africa	Asia	South America
15	Sahara	Gobi	Negev	Mojave	Bermuda

Word Games • 6–8 © 2005 Creative Teaching Press

Name _____ Date _____

More Odd Word Out

VOCABULARY

In each row, find and circle the word that does not belong. Be able to explain why it does not belong with the other words. Use a dictionary if you need help.

1 hexagon	rhombus	rumba	cube	octagon
2 Chile	Panama	Bolivia	Peru	Venezuela
3 hurricane	tsunami	tornado	cycle	cyclone
4 sepal	stamen	rock	root	pistil
5 should	were	might	have	buy
6 nor	alas	oh	ugh	ouch
7 caliper	thermometer	scale	barometer	stapler
8 Germany	Italy	Fiji	Ireland	France
9 civet	ibex	katydid	okapi	cheetah
10 mile	gallon	degree	pint	bottle
11 mamba	samba	krait	python	anaconda
12 Arctic	India	Indian	Pacific	Atlantic
13 tadpole	comment	windmill	icecap	beside
14 high	area	paper	ruler	noon
15 auk	curlew	swallow	egret	regret

Word Games • 6–8 © 2005 Creative Teaching Press

Riddle #1

Synonyms, Adjectives, Syllables, Interjections, and Conjunctions

How does the man in the moon cut his hair?

Follow the directions to find the answer to the riddle. Then circle the words that have not been crossed out. Read the answer going down from top to bottom starting in the upper left-hand corner of the chart. Write the answer to the riddle on the line.

VERSATILE	ALAS	BRAISE	POACH
INFORMATION	NOR	BEAUTIFUL	ECLIPSE
OUCH	TUMULT	VIOLET	JUBILANT
NEITHER	BAH	ELIGIBLE	IT
LILAC	OR	PLUM	OH
BUT	BARBECUE	AND	MAUVE
RUCKUS	DORMITORY	BEDLAM	HYPOTENUSE

- Cross off all words that are shades of the color *purple*.
- Cross off all words that are synonyms for the word *cook*.
- Cross off all words that are synonyms for the word *noise*.
- Cross off all words that are adjectives.
- Cross off all words that have exactly four syllables.
- Cross off all words that are interjections.
- Cross off all words that are conjunctions.

Answer to Riddle

_____

Riddle #2

Synonyms, Prepositions, Past Participles, Suffixes, and Science

What did one earthquake say to the other earthquake?

Follow the directions to find the answer to the riddle. Then circle the words that have not been crossed off. Read the answer going down from top to bottom starting in the upper left-hand corner of the chart. Write the answer to the riddle on the line.

OVER	CUP	GREBE	SCAMPER
QUETZAL	AFFLUENT	ROOM	BEEN
RISEN	IT'S	OPULENT	STURGEON
HAND	BENEATH	DASH	LUXURIOUS
SCURRY	GONE	NOT	FAULT
BASS	PROSPEROUS	FLEE	GIVEN
AMONG	HADDOCK	MY	WREN

- Cross off all words that are synonyms for the word *rich*.
- Cross off all words that are synonyms for the word *run*.
- Cross off all words that are prepositions.
- Cross off all words that are names of birds.
- Cross off all words that are names of fishes.
- Cross off all words that that are past participle forms of verbs.
- Cross off all words that could end with the suffix *-ful*.

Answer to Riddle

_____

Word Games • 6–8 © 2005 Creative Teaching Press

Name _____ Date _____

Riddle #3

Pronouns, Adverbs, Synonyms, and Science

What would you get if a pig learned karate?

Follow the directions to find the answer to the riddle. Then circle the words that have not been crossed off. Read the answer going down from top to bottom starting in the upper left-hand corner of the chart. Write the answer to the riddle on the line.

BAWLED	RATHER	COLONY	COCCYX
COBRA	PYTHON	AMUSING	DEDICATED
LUDICROUS	FLOCK	HERD	CHOPS
WAILED	FEMUR	YOURS	COPPERHEAD
ULNA	WHIMPERED	HASTILY	HILARIOUS
SHE	PORK	VIPER	NOWHERE
HIGH	HIS	PATELLA	SOBBED

- Cross off all words that are pronouns.
- Cross off all words that are adverbs.
- Cross off all words that are synonyms for the word *cried*.
- Cross off all words that are synonyms of the word *funny*.
- Cross off all words that are names of snakes.
- Cross off all words that are names of bones in the human body.
- Cross off all words that begin and end with the same letter.
- Cross off all words that are names of animal groups.

Answer to Riddle

_____

Word Games • 6–8 © 2005 Creative Teaching Press

Riddle #4

Syllables, Suffixes, Plurals, Synonyms, Compound Words, and Prefixes

What is something that all students have seen but will never see again?

Follow the directions to find the answer to the riddle. Then circle the words that have not been crossed off. Read the answer going down from top to bottom starting in the upper left-hand corner of the chart. Write the answer to the riddle on the line.

LONE	QUALIFICATION	COMPLEX	TEDIOUS
DATA	CUSPID	MEN	ENTERTAIN
FOCAL	FOREVER	TRADEMARK	CENTENNIAL
BRIEFCASE	ENTANGLE	AWE	ENGAGE
GOVERN	FULFILL	YESTERDAY	LARVAE
CHILDREN	ANNUAL	UNNECESSARY	EYELID
ARDOUS	CACTI	ENJOY	CYCLE

- Cross off all words that have exactly five syllables.
- Cross off all words that could end in the suffix -*some*.
- Cross off all words that could end in the suffix -*ment*.
- Cross off all words that are plural forms of nouns.
- Cross off all words that are compound words.
- Cross off all words that are synonyms of the word difficult.
- Cross off all words that could have the prefix *bi*-.

Answer to Riddle

_____

Word Games • 6–8 © 2005 Creative Teaching Press

Answer Key

Answers will vary. Possible answers include:

area
arson
arts
blob
blot
blots
bomb
bombs
bore
born
borne
both
city
cut
cuts
earn
ears
eats
fist
gage
garage
gear
gears
gene
genre
gray
great
icy
lobs
lone
loner
loners
lost
lots
mist
misty
mobs
more
moron
most
motor
motors
near
nearer
nears
oboe
rage

rear
robot
robots
robs
rotor
rotors
rots
sits
sobs
sort
sorts
stag
stare
stay
stone
storage
story
stray
tore
torn
tray
treat
treats
tutor
tutors

Word Square #2 (page 6)

Answers will vary. Possible answers include:

again
ages
aging
ailing
angel
angle
angles
cage
cages
cans
cart
crack
cracks
crane
cranes
craw
gain
gaining
gains
gigs
gins

gnat
goes
inks
knack
knacks
liar
line
linen
lines
lining
linings
link
links
logo
logs
nags
nine
nines
quack
quacks
quart
quiz
rack
racks
rain
raining
rains
range
ranges
ranging
scar
scat
snack
snacks
snag
snags
tack
tacks
tags
tartar
track
tracks
train
trains
twin
twins
wage
wages
wags
wail
wailing

wane
wanes
waning
wart
wigs
wine
wines
wink
winks
zigs
zinc

Word Square #3 (page 7)

Answers will vary. Possible answers include:

ants
antsy
aster
asters
bean
beast
beasts
beat
beats
bench
bent
bets
blue
blurt
blurts
bulk
burst
bursts
cent
cents
century
cheat
cheater
cheaters
cheats
cherub
east
eater
eaters
eats
heat
heater
heaters
heats
hers
hulk

hurt
hurts
huts
lube
lure
lute
nasty
neat
neater
nets
oats
rent
renter
renters
retreat
ruts
sate
stat
stats
strut
struts
stub
taste
taster
tasters
teas
tent
tents
toast
toaster
toasters
toasts
toasty
treat
treats
trench
true
tryst
tube
tuber
tubers
wire
wiry
wren

Word Square #4 (page 8)

Answers will vary. Possible answers include:

again
against
aged
aging
airs
aping
axing
axle
dune
dusk
dust
dusts
ended
exist
exists
exit
exits
gain
gaining
gains
gaping
gene
gigs
glen
glens
gnus
inks
junk
junks
just
knit
knits
legend
legs
lend
paged
pain
pains
pair
pairing
pairs
pigs
ping
pings
pink
pins
rigs
rings
rink

rinks
risk
risks
sign
signs
singe
singed
single
sink
sinks
skunk
skunks
snit
snits
stair
stairs
sting
stings
string
stringed
strings
suns
tags
taping
tapings
tapir
tapirs
taxi
ting
tinge
tingle
tins
trip
unsung
wring
wringing
wrings
wrist
wrists
writ
writs

Round and Round (page 9)

Answers will vary. Possible answers include:

able
air
ale
amp
back
bale
bam
banal
bay
black
cab
cable
cam
can
canal
cane
car
cay
ear
earn
kale
lab
lack
lair
lam
lamp
lap
law
lay
leak
lean
leap
male
man
mane
map
mar
may
nap
nay
pack
pair
pale
pan
par
rack
ram
ramp
ran

rap
raw
ray
wan
war
way
yak
yap
yarn

Round and Round Again (page 10)

Answers will vary. Possible answers include:

ace
aces
ache
aches
are
area
car
care
cares
cars
chest
chests
each
ear
ears
emit
emits
hear
hears
hearse
hem
hemp
here
its
mere
met
meter
meters
mite
miter
mites
pea
peach
peaches
pear
pears
per
pest

pester
pesters
pests
pet
pets
race
racer
racers
reach
reaches
rear
rears
rehearse
rehearses
remit
remits
reset
resets
rest
rests
retest
retests
sea
sear
sears
set
sets
stem
teach
teacher
teachers
teaches
test
tester
testers
tests
time
timer
timers
times
zest

Zig Zag (page 11)

Answers will vary. Possible answers include:

are
arm
army
dam
dare
dared
day
dead
dear
desk
desks
did
dip
disk
disks
dodo
dot
ear
edit
idea
ides
ink
inks
kid
kids
kin
kink
kinks
kit
made
mar
mare
mares
may
nip
nit
oar
ode
odes
pin
pink
pit
ray
read
reader
reads
red
reds
sea

seam
sin
sip
sis
sit
skin
skip
skit
tide
tides
tin
tip
toad
toads
toy

More Zig Zag (page 12)

Answers will vary. Possible answers include:

arc
are
area
ark
bar
bare
bark
barking
bra
broke
broken
coke
colt
core
cork
corking
crab
ear
engine
era
gig
gilt
gin
high
hike
hiker
hilt
hit
ilk
ink
inking
kilt

king
kink
kit
knit
light
lighting
like
liken
liking
line
linen
liner
ling
lining
link
linking
lit
lore
night
nil
nine
nit
orb
ore
thigh
thing
think
thinking
tight
tike
tilt
tilting
tin
ting

Star Burst (page 13)

Answers will vary. Possible answers include:

and
ant
ants
art
arts
dad
dart
darts
data
end
ewe
hole
holes
hose
hoses
host
hosts
lend
lent
lose
lost
nest
nests
new
pen
pent
pep
pest
pests
pew
ran
rant
rants
rat
rats
send
sent
sew
slew
stand
star
start
starts
stat
stats
tad
tan
tar
wend

went
west

Diamond Puzzle (page 14)

Answers will vary. Possible answers include:

aorta
aortas
ash
ashen
atop
cad
cads
case
cases
cast
casts
cat
cats
coat
coats
cop
cot
cots
coup
court
courts
dad
dads
data
ewe
ewes
hen
hew
hews
mum
nest
nests
new
news
oat
oats
our
pock
pop
port
ports
pot
potato
pour
road

115

roads
rock
rot
rots
rum
rump
sack
sad
sew
sews
stack
stir
stock
stop
tack
tad
toad
toast
toasts
top
tot
tots
west
wit
wits

Hidden Ant (page 15)

1. truant
2. banter
3. antelope
4. elegant
5. currant
6. anthem
7. distant
8. restaurant
9. guarantee
10. brilliant
11. abundant
12. anthology

Hidden Art (page 16)

1. quart
2. article
3. particle
4. spartan
5. arthropod
6. braggart
7. articulate
8. partition
9. martial
10. artificial
11. compartment
12. kindergarten

Hidden Cat (page 17)

1. category
2. scatter
3. vacate
4. location
5. delicate
6. complicated
7. indicate
8. cattle
9. intricate
10. catalyst
11. fabrication
12. catastrophe

Hidden Mat (page 18)

1. matter
2. mature
3. formation
4. ultimate
5. matinee
6. diplomat
7. matrimony
8. primate
9. maternal
10. grammatical

Hidden Men (page 19)

1. menace
2. mention
3. momentary
4. amendment
5. mendicant
6. document
7. implement
8. compliment
9. appointment
10. increment
11. replacement
12. complement

Hidden Pan (page 20)

1. panic
2. panther
3. company
4. pantry
5. companion
6. expanse
7. pancreas
8. panorama
9. spangle
10. pandemonium

Hidden Pen (page 21)

1. pensive
2. serpent
3. pennant
4. appendix
5. peninsula
6. expensive
7. penetrate
8. pendulum
9. independent
10. compensate

Hidden Rat (page 22)

1. ratio
2. ratify
3. strategy
4. ration
5. berate
6. rattle
7. exaggerate
8. marathon
9. decorate
10. registration

Hidden Tan (page 23)

1. tangle
2. tangy
3. standard
4. constant
5. tantrum
6. tangerine
7. resistance
8. acceptance
9. important
10. orangutan
11. metropolitan
12. tantalize

Hidden Ten (page 24)

1. attend
2. tension
3. often
4. tendon
5. pretense
6. tendril
7. intense
8. tenement
9. potential
10. tendency

Bird Search (page 25)

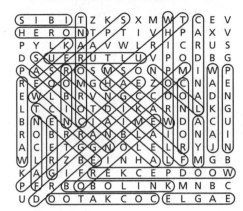

Bone Search (page 26)

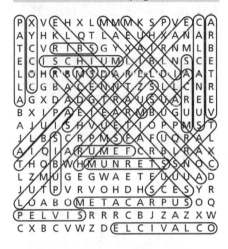

Color Search (page 27)

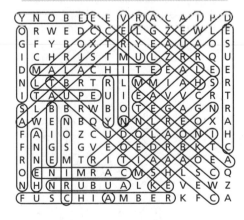

Flower Search (page 28)

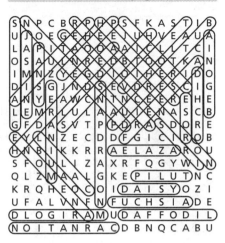

Health and Nutrition Search (page 29)

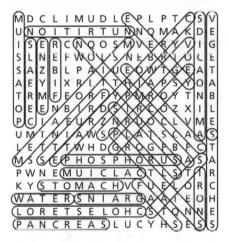

Mammal Search (page 30)

Solar System Search (page 31)

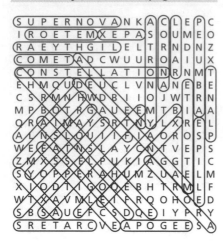

Nations of Africa Search (page 34)

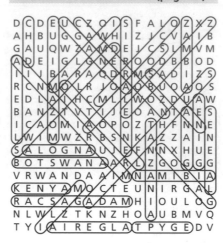

Occupation Search (page 37)

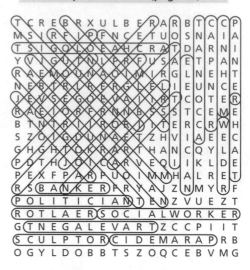

Weather Search (page 32)

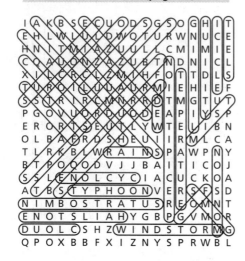

Nations of Asia Search (page 35)

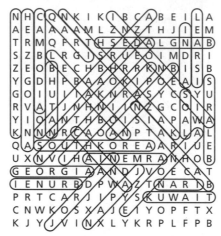

President Search (page 38)

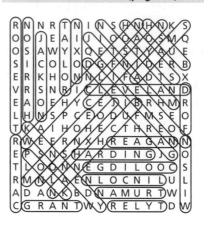

Capital Search (page 33)

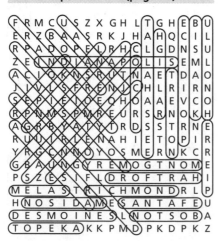

Nations of Europe Search (page 36)

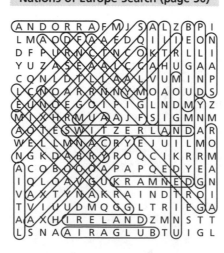

State Search (page 39)

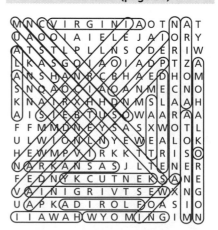

Things that Travel on Water (page 40)

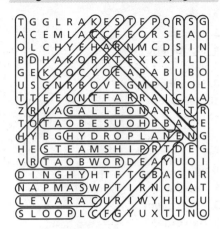

Pick a Word (page 41)

Answers will vary.

Suffixes (page 42)

Answers will vary.

Syllable Count (page 43)

Answers will vary.

Parts of Speech (page 44)

Answers will vary.

Geography (page 45)

Answers will vary.

People (page 46)

Answers will vary.

Living Things (page 47)

Answers will vary.

Foods (page 48)

Answers will vary.

Shopping Spree (page 49)

Answers will vary.

Odds and Ends (page 50)

Answers will vary.

Synonym Puzzle (page 51)

Across
2. limp
4. peculiar
6. obvious
8. timid
10. blank
12. taunt
14. gigantic

Down
1. rival
3. plead
5. peril
7. reimburse
9. abrupt
11. fierce
13. adjust
15. dubious

Antonym Puzzle (page 52)

Across
2. permanent
4. rude
6. fragile
8. simple
10. harmful
12. shallow

Down
1. plentiful
3. resist
5. inferior
7. maximum
9. idle
11. include
13. allow
14. flimsy
15. vague

Homophone Puzzle (page 53)

Across
2. plumb
4. idle
6. yolk
8. auricle
10. heir
12. aloud
14. barren
15. isle

Down
1. links
3. beech
5. dual
7. counsel
9. gored
11. bridal
13. clause

Noun Puzzle (page 54)

Across
2. flair
4. enthusiasm
6. armada
8. epic
10. notion
12. stature
14. lentil
15. zephyr

Down
1. creed
3. assumption
5. palate
7. incident
9. obelisk
11. decree
13. token

Plural Puzzle (page 55)

Across

2. oxen
4. deer
6. octopuses
8. wharves
10. skies
12. feet
14. calves
15. sopranos

Down

1. moose
3. taxes
5. ratios
7. guesses
9. daisies
11. studios
13. salmon

Adjective Puzzle (page 56)

Across

2. hazy
4. turbulent
6. irritable
8. deft
10. fanciful
12. concise
13. savage
14. reluctant

Down

1. bizarre
3. jubilant
5. humble
6. influential
7. askew
9. immaculate
11. sultry

Verb Puzzle (page 57)

Across

2. narrate
4. drench
6. assemble
8. repeal
10. gush
12. forge
14. subside
15. hover

Down

1. engulf
3. budge
5. petrify
7. bawl
9. stagger
11. heckle
13. submerge

Past Participle Puzzle (page 58)

Across

2. drawn
4. gone
6. frozen
8. shrunk
10. taken
12. seen
14. written

Down

1. ridden
3. sung
5. sprung
7. worn
9. eaten
11. shaken
13. flown
15. known

Abbreviation Puzzle (page 59)

Across

2. avenue
4. Lieutenant
6. yard
8. September
10. teaspoon
12. junior

Down

1. Tuesday
3. department
5. boulevard
7. Governor
9. Thursday
11. paid
13. tablespoon
14. parkway
15. corporation

State Capitals Puzzle (page 60)

Across

2. Concord
4. Sacramento
6. Atlanta
8. Boston
10. Pierre
12. Topeka
14. Columbus
15. Springfield

Down

1. Dover
3. Boise
5. Hartford
7. Nashville
9. Austin
11. Phoenix
13. Salem

Animal Offspring Puzzle (page 61)

Across
2. fawn
4. eaglet
5. pup
7. calf
9. cub
11. cygnet
12. shoat
13. kitten
14. kit

Down
1. whelp
3. colt
5. poult
6. fry
8. gosling
10. chick

Science Puzzle (page 62)

Across
2. atmosphere
4. humidity
6. rotate
8. reflection
10. invertebrate
12. weather
14. density

Down
1. insulator
3. amphibian
5. tendon
7. corona
9. capillaries
11. tissue
13. vertebrate
15. neutron

Insect Puzzle (page 63)

Across
2. larva
4. six
6. caterpillar
8. feelers
10. termite
12. cocoon

Down
1. colony
3. cricket
5. wasp
7. flea
9. thorax
11. change
13. three
14. swarm
15. two

Number, Please (page 64)

Across
2. sixteen
4. ten
6. sixty
8. three
10. seven
12. nine
14. two

Down
1. sixty
3. one hundred
5. twenty four
7. twenty
9. four
11. twelve
13. six
15. eight

What Would You Do with an Apiary? (page 65)

1. d
2. a
3. d
4. c
5. b
6. c
7. c
8. a
9. b
10. d

What Would You Do with a Buoy? (page 66)

1. c
2. c
3. b
4. a
5. b
6. c
7. a
8. d
9. c
10. a

What Would You Do with a Dais? (page 67)

1. d
2. a
3. c
4. b
5. d
6. c
7. d
8. b
9. d
10. a

What Would You Do with a Fathom? (page 68)

1. c
2. d
3. a
4. d
5. c
6. b
7. a
8. c
9. b
10. d

What Would You Do with a Nozzle? (page 71)

1. b
2. b
3. a
4. d
5. c
6. d
7. b
8. d
9. c
10. d

What Would You Do with a Vandal? (page 74)

1. b
2. c
3. a
4. d
5. c
6. d
7. a
8. a
9. d
10. b

What Would You Do with a Kiwi? (page 69)

1. a
2. d
3. d
4. c
5. c
6. a
7. c
8. d
9. b
10. d

What Would You Do with a Scull? (page 72)

1. d
2. b
3. d
4. a
5. d
6. a
7. c
8. a
9. d
10. c

Ladder Links #1 (page 75)

#1
home
some
same
came
camp
carp
cart

#2
loon
loan
load
road
read
head
hear

What Would You Do with a Larder? (page 70)

1. b
2. a
3. d
4. c
5. b
6. a
7. c
8. d
9. b
10. a

What Would You Do with a Torrent? (page 73)

1. c
2. a
3. d
4. b
5. d
6. a
7. b
8. d
9. c
10. a

Ladder Links #2 (page 76)

#1
sack
lack
lace
pace
pane
pine
pint

#2
paper
caper
capes
copes
cores
cords
words

Ladder Links #3 (page 77)

#1
hurl
hurt
curt
cure
care
came
fame
tame

#2
lint
lint
line
lice
rice
dice
dime

Ladder Links #4 (page 78)

#1
bend
send
sand
sane
same
came
game

#2
pick
pack
rack
race
rake
rate
gate

Ladder Links #5 (page 79)

#1
book
boot
boat
coat
goat
moat
meat

#2
host
cost
cast
case
cake
take
bake
bike

Ladder Links #6 (page 80)

#1	**#3**
never	blend
lever	bleed
liver	breed
lives	bread
limes	tread
times	treat

#2	**#4**
hard	story
ward	stork
wand	stark
wane	shark
cane	sharp
case	
ease	

Ladder Links #7 (page 81)

#1	**#3**
chew	novel
chow	hovel
show	hover
slow	cover
slew	covet
sled	comet

#2	**#4**
blank	boom
bland	loom
brand	loam
braid	foam
brain	foal
grain	foil
	soil

Ladder Links #8 (page 82)

#1
beat
meat
melt
malt
male
mane

#3
truce
truck
trick
brick
brisk

#2
warm
ward
card
cord
cold

#4
goad
glad
clad
clap
flap
flip
clip

Ladder Links #9 (page 83)

#1
tool
toil
foil
fail
fall
ball
bale

#3
scene
scent
scant
slant
plant

#2
sage
page
pale
pall
wall
well

#4
dart
dare
dame
dome
home
hole
sole

Ladder Links #10 (page 84)

#1
coal
foal
fool
food
fond
find
fine

#3
write
trite
tribe
bribe
brine
brink
drink

#2
whale
shale
share
shore
spore
sport
spout

#4
hook
look
loot
loft
lift
sift

Noun Analogies (page 85)

1. d
2. a
3. c
4. b
5. a
6. d
7. b
8. d
9. b
10. c

Verb Analogies (page 86)

1. c
2. b
3. a
4. c
5. d
6. a
7. b
8. a
9. d
10. a

Adjective Analogies (page 87)

1. c
2. d
3. b
4. a
5. d
6. b
7. b
8. d
9. b
10. a

Analogy Challenge #1 (page 88)

1. b
2. d
3. a
4. b
5. c
6. a
7. b
8. d
9. c
10. c

Analogy Challenge #2 (page 89)

1. c
2. c
3. c
4. a
5. b
6. d
7. b
8. a
9. d
10. b

Analogy Challenge #3 (page 90)

1. a
2. c
3. b
4. b
5. d
6. c
7. b
8. d
9. a
10. c

Analogy Challenge #4 (page 91)

1. c
2. a
3. d
4. b
5. d
6. d
7. a
8. c
9. a
10. d

Synonym and Antonym Analogies (page 92)

1. a
2. d
3. d
4. b
5. d
6. a
7. b
8. d
9. b
10. a

On the Menu Analogies (page 93)

1. b
2. d
3. a
4. c
5. b
6. d
7. b
8. a
9. b
10. d

Sports Analogies (page 94)

1. c
2. b
3. a
4. c
5. b
6. d
7. d
8. d
9. a
10. c

What's Hot?—What's Not? #1 (page 95)

1. all are compound words
2. all are adverbs
3. all are pronouns
4. all are prepositions
5. all are past tense form of a verb
6. all describe how things taste
7. all start and end with the same letter of the alphabet
8. all are words with only one syllable
9. all are present tense verbs
10. all are spelled the same going forward and backward (palindromes)

What's Hot?—What's Not? #2 (page 96)

1. all are names of flowers
2. all are shades of the color red
3. all are synonyms for the word old
4. all are names of things that hold something
5. all are names of dances
6. all are dry measures
7. all are forms of metamorphic rocks; all are names of rocks
8. all are things that have holes
9. all are baseball terms
10. all are names of mammals

Continent, Please (page 97)	Geography Guru (page 98)

Continent, Please (page 97)

North America
Barbados
Belize
Canada
Costa Rica
Cuba
Mexico
Nicaragua

South America
Argentina
Bolivia
Chile
Guyana
Peru
Venezuela

Asia
Lebanon
Nepal
Oman
Pakistan
Turkey
Vietnam

Europe
Andorra
Austria
Czech Republic
Greece
Liechtenstein
Poland

Africa
Algeria
Benin
Chad
Djibouti
Ghana
Lesotho

Geography Guru (page 98)

city
Los Angeles
Boston
Denver
Dallas
Santa Fe
Baltimore

state
Florida
Illinois
Tennessee
Montana
Rhode Island
Utah

country
China
England
Brazil
Japan
Kenya
Israel

continent
North America
South America
Antarctica
Africa
Asia
Europe

mammal
gnu
koala
coyote
yak
sloth
hyena

reptile
tortoise
cobra
lizard
copperhead
crocodile
alligator

bird
heron
flamingo
condor
raven
toucan
nightingale

fish
trout
salmon
mackerel
guppy
minnow
barracuda

Word Wizard (page 100)

noun
errand
California
happiness
signature
table
house

verb
is
yawned
had
extinguished
should
recommend

adjective
frightened
two
those
three
new
incredible

adverb
regularly
away
upstairs
sarcastically
tomorrow
immediately

Five-Letter Anagrams (page 101)

1. glare
2. votes
3. snips
4. wipes
5. march
6. field
7. dozen
8. there
9. ports
10. canoe
11. quite
12. sores

Six-Letter Anagrams (page 102)

1. melons
2. vetoed
3. citrus
4. secure
5. things
6. nicest
7. finder
8. dashed
9. braved
10. sauces
11. resist
12. dealer

Seven-Letter Anagrams (page 103)

1. reverse
2. rentals
3. fitness
4. ripples
5. relayed
6. resells
7. license
8. section
9. treason
10. thicken
11. reheats
12. markers

Eight-Letter Anagrams (page 104)

1. charming
2. sunlight
3. teaching
4. imprints
5. relation
6. nameless
7. lessened
8. listened
9. roasting
10. weathers
11. recitals
12. infringe

Odd Word Out (page 105)

1. palmetto—not a flower
2. none—not a preposition
3. skate—not a color
4. pretext—not a part of a book
5. huddle—not an ice hockey term
6. cuddle—not a cooking term
7. coal—not an igneous rock
8. pullet—not a type of machine
9. plane—not an astronomy term
10. patio—not a type of shelter or dwelling
11. Kenya—not the name of a river
12. since—not a pronoun
13. Jasper—not a Canadian province or territory
14. New Zealand—not a continent
15. Bermuda—not the name of a desert

More Odd Word Out (page 106)

1. rumba—not a geometric shape
2. Panama—not a country in South America
3. cycle—not a type of severe storm or weather condition
4. rock—not a part of a flower
5. buy—not a helping verb
6. nor—not an interjection
7. stapler—not a device that measures something
8. Fiji—not a country in Europe
9. katydid—not a type of mammal
10. bottle—not a unit of measurement
11. samba—not a type of snake
12. India—not the name of an ocean
13. comment—not a compound word
14. paper—doesn't start and end with the same letter of the alphabet
15. regret—not the name of a bird

Riddle #1 (page 107)

eclipse it

Riddle #2 (page 108)

It's not my fault.

Riddle #3 (page 109)

pork chops

Riddle #4 (page 110)

yesterday